FIND INSPIRATION AND TRANSFORMATION
THROUGH THE INSIGHTS OF OTHERS

A multi-author anthology
compiled by

OYINLOLA BUKKY AKANDE

THE LENSES OF LIFE

Find Inspiration and Transformation through the Insights of Others

A multi-author anthology compiled by Oyinlola Bukky Akande

Published by
O • B • A Connections Ltd.
Email: obaconnections@gmail.com
Telephone: +44 (0) 7984 260 508
Website: www.obaconnections.com

First published 2025

ISBN: 978-1-0682307-2-1

Cover/book design by Imaginovation Ltd.

Printed in the United Kingdom.

Contents

Dedication

To God, the giver of wisdom and vision. Thank You for being the source of all inspiration.

To every reader who desires to grow through the stories and insights of others, may these pages stir something within you.

To the contributors, thank you for lending your voice, your wisdom, and your journey to this work. Each of you has poured into these pages from a place of grace. Your words are a gift, and your willingness to share them will light the way for many.

Acknowledgments

I extend my heartfelt gratitude to every contributor whose reflections have shaped this work. To our families, friends, and church communities, thank you for your unwavering support and prayers throughout this journey. Special thanks to our readers: your willingness to engage with these stories gives meaning to this publication.

To Tolu Shofule, whose design brilliance brought life to the pages, I say 'thank you'. Your work goes far beyond aesthetics; it reflects deep thought, intentionality, and excellence. You captured the essence of *The Lenses of Life* and gave it form. This book would not carry the same presence without your creative input.

I also express my sincere gratitude to the editorial team – Bayo Ukas, Iwuese Akuhwa, Kike Adebiyi, Olutunu Babalola-Daniel, Joy Eseose Usiabulu, and Emmanuel Victor Opasola – for their invaluable contributions.

Special thanks to Mike Adeyele, who led the media team with excellence, and to Eliyo Ajiboye, our dedicated project manager, for overseeing every detail of this work.

Above all, to the Almighty God – our Source, Sustainer, and Saviour – be all the glory, honour, and praise.

Introduction

Every now and then, we are gifted with the wisdom of those who have walked the road before us, those whose experiences, and insights help light our own path. Lenses of Life is one of such gifts.

This book is a carefully curated compilation of perspectives from accomplished individuals, people who have lived, learned, and leaned into life with intention. Across its three sections, Insightful, Impactful, and Eye Opener, you will find stories, truths, and lessons shaped by experience, sharpened by exposure, and offered with humility.

The purpose of this book is simple but powerful: to impact lives through shared knowledge. These authors write not from theory, but from practice. Their lenses are not borrowed; they are earned. And with each chapter, they open a window for you to see something new about life, growth, purpose, and yourself.

As you read, allow each piece to meet you where you are. Reflect deeply. Question gently. Grow freely.

The *Lenses of Life* was written for you.

PART ONE

INSIGHT

2

CHAPTER 1

SOCIETAL PRESSURE INSIGHT

(Observing how societal pressures impact individual choices)

Understanding its impact and developing coping strategies is crucial in a world where societal pressure shapes our choices and behaviors. Societal pressure refers to the influence exerted by society on individuals to conform to certain behaviors, beliefs, or standards. These pressures are expectations that affect whole communities or specific parts of them, such as the pressure to marry or have children. Today, we are free to hold our opinions, but we often face restrictions when acting on them. Societal pressure is the influence individuals feel from others in their social circles or society to act, think, or behave in particular ways. It can encourage positive actions, like being kind or working hard. Still, it can also push individuals toward negative behaviors, such as conforming to harmful norms or engaging in risky activities just to fit in. Essentially, it is the push and pull we all experience from the people and culture around us, shaping our actions and decisions—sometimes even without our realization.

- Social pressure encourages people to try to fit in with those around them. Sometimes, fitting in may come naturally, but in other cases, people may need to change their views, choices, and outlooks to avoid being the odd one out. This innate inclination towards social conformity isn't just about immediate social comfort; it's deeply rooted in our evolutionary past. Humans depend on one another as a species—while other organisms may thrive in solitude, we survive best when living in a community. Consequently, we have evolved to seek conformity to ensure social harmony and mutual survival. Adapting to shared norms and values helps us integrate into our social groups, making us more likely to receive support and cooperation from others. In essence, our survival and success as a species have been significantly influenced by our ability to conform to the group expectations of our communities.

- Societal pressure, a potent force shaped by society's norms and expectations, significantly influences our behavior and mental well-being. This external pressure, varying across life stages and cultural contexts, affects everything from personal relationships to career choices. It manifests in various forms, from explicit expectations to implicit norms that dictate 'acceptable' behavior. This pressure can also lead to anxiety symptoms and a tendency to conform, impacting young adults and adults alike. It's essential to examine how these societal norms have evolved and how they continue to make people see themselves through a lens of negativity.

- Exploring the psychological aspects of societal pressure reveals why it's such a pervasive force. The need for social acceptance and the fear of rejection are deeply ingrained in human psychology. Societal pressure exploits these needs, often leading individuals to behave or adopt beliefs that align with societal norms, even if they conflict with personal values. This can create pressure that leads individuals to feel compelled to conform, often sacrificing their individuality and mental health. Social comparison, a natural human instinct, can become a double-edged sword when influenced by societal pressure. It frequently results in negative self-assessment and an ongoing sense of not measuring up to others. This comparison can heighten feelings of inadequacy and contribute to mental health issues such as anxiety and depression. Recognizing and managing the propensity for social comparison is vital in lessening the adverse effects of societal pressure.

- Societal pressure evolves with each life stage, presenting unique challenges and expectations. Young adults often face intense societal pressure as they navigate major life transitions, such as choosing a career path or establishing personal relationships. This period is marked by a heightened sensitivity to societal expectations and a strong desire to conform. As individuals progress into adulthood, societal pressure shifts focus, often centering around career success, family life, and social status. The nature of the pressure may change, but its impact on mental health and well-being remains significant.

- Developing resilience and a strong sense of self is key to mitigating the adverse effects of societal pressure. Embracing individualism involves recognizing and valuing one's unique qualities and life path and resisting the urge to conform to unrealistic societal standards. Building resilience involves developing a strong, positive self-image and the ability to bounce back from setbacks. This can be achieved through self-reflection, mindfulness practices, and seeking support from friends, family, or mental health professionals. Individuals can navigate societal pressure more effectively by fostering a mindset that values personal authenticity over societal conformity.

- Social norms sometimes influence major life decisions such as how to treat people, what career path to take, how to vote, and when and whom to marry. Humans can be social creatures, and we tend to live social lives in community with others. Social pressure regarding how to behave, what to do, what to wear, and dozens of other facets of our lives are all around us and can influence our choices and how we make those choices. It can also affect how we construct our own identities and whether we honor our uniqueness. Sometimes, the desire to conform and please others can affect our emotional health and ability to have healthy relationships with others or ourselves.

It is interesting to know that when the world only had two people, Adam and Eve, they were not spared from societal pressure; Adam and Eve influenced Adam. God also influenced them, and eventually, the devil influenced them. When God placed these two, Adam and Eve, in the Garden of Eden, He gave them instructions, the most important of which was that, as much as they could eat from every tree in the garden, there were two in the middle or center of the garden which they cannot eat from, namely, the tree of the Knowledge of good and evil, the second being, the tree of life. In his guide, Adam added to this instruction, telling his wife Eve not to go near or touch the tree and that she would not eat from it. The devil came along and convinced Eve to touch it, examine it, and see its beauty and the transformation it would bring to her; she was convinced and gave in to eat it and eventually gave it to her husband, Adam, who was with her. We could see how the first community played out, how each other was trying to fit in and live pleasing each other, with the peak being the man pleasing his wife. Apostle Paul would come to the millennials later to help us understand that Eve was deceived, which suggests that Adam was not confused but probably wanted to follow his wife.

The world has now developed so rapidly, and different customs and traditions have shaped the mentality of generations, although there are the oriental culture and the Occidental culture. The oriental culture is the culture from the East, while the Occidental culture is the culture from the West. Values and traditions characterize Eastern cultures, and superstitions abound within them, while Western cultures believe more in seeking wisdom, principles, and facts. Apostle Paul summarized this in the first chapter of his epistle to the Corinthians church: the Greeks seek wisdom while the Jews seek signs. The Greeks were the image of the Occidental culture, while the Jews were the image of the oriental culture. How we think, act, and behave is mainly due to these two kinds of cultural prevalence. The pressure that dominates your society is shaped by the cultural views prevalent in your locality and community.

The Yoruba culture, to which I am connected, is an Eastern tradition. It is believed that they are migrants from the Arabian Peninsula, which is reflected in their beliefs; we have many superstitions and place significant value on tradition and mysticism. We live a communal lifestyle where everyone in the neighborhood shares everything.

Christianity has also aligned us with Western culture; we cannot underestimate the influence of the West on religion. Western education has opened our eyes to understanding their ways and norms, where principles guide ideologies. Capitalism is the prevailing system in the West, where people build upon empirical evidence rather than superstitions. This has fostered innovations and different mentalities across generations.

Changing perspectives in Eastern cultures is nearly impossible, resulting in societal pressure in these cultures to become traditional and conservative. There is a specific way society operates, which everyone must conform to, as all are striving to meet societal expectations. Although there may be slight differences between Eastern and Western cultures, which adds pressure on individuals, evidence of societal pressure exists in both realms. No one is immune to the significant impact of society on their life. With the rise of social media, we have also recognized that virtual communities significantly influence individual pressure.

Social media platforms, especially those popular among young adults, have become significant sources of societal pressure. They often showcase idealized, picture-perfect lives, creating unrealistic personal success and happiness standards. This leads to increased social comparison, as individuals feel compelled to evaluate their lives against these idealized online images, often experiencing feelings of inadequacy or anxiety. The pressure to present a perfect life on platforms like Instagram can distort one's sense of reality and negatively affect mental health. The dangers of TikTok are evident; many countries are imposing bans on these social media platforms due to their impact on the younger generation.

I believe the fundamental issue facing humanity can be traced back to sin, and the earliest manifestation of this sin is underlying the societal pressure for acceptance. Self-centeredness leads to positive and negative outcomes. Our selfishness is a core reason for societal pressure, or perhaps this pressure exists independently. Everyone wants to be seen as better than their neighbors; we seek validation and strive to be valued in society. Whether in Eastern or Western cultures, people often display desires driven by the lust of the eyes, the flesh, and the pride of life. These traits of a fallen world compel individuals to exert pressure on themselves. People can be materialistic and egotistical; the ego embodies pride in self-preservation and maintaining one's image. We often overlook that materialism does not truly define us; regardless of our status, we are all born the same way, and death is an inevitable reality.

In Eastern cultures, women are frequently perceived as lesser than their male counterparts, while Western cultures typically afford them more respect. A girl born in the Eastern world faces pressure from the beginning; traditionally, a man with only daughters is not regarded highly. Even today, women aged 30 to 40 are often considered "late" for marriage, placing immense pressure on young women to marry before 30, ideally to a financially stable partner. Men are traditionally viewed as the breadwinners, compelling young men to aim for success before reaching 30 years old. The Western world's influence has significantly contributed to the decline of boys' schools, eventually allowing girls access to education.

Societal pressure can manifest in many forms, including peer pressure, academic stress, family expectations, social media influence, pressure to conform to beauty standards, pressure to adopt a particular lifestyle, pressure to engage in risky behaviours, and pressure regarding career choices.

All these pressures stem from the desire to fit in and meet societal expectations, reflecting any influence exerted by a community or group to promote specific behaviors or beliefs among individuals. This societal pressure can profoundly impact individuals by shaping their behavior, beliefs, and self-esteem, often driving them to conform to societal norms even when they clash with their values. This can lead to stress, anxiety, and even depression, particularly when individuals feel pressured to meet unrealistic expectations regarding appearance, career, or social status. Such pressure can manifest in various ways, such as altering one's style to fit in, making choices based on others' opinions, or suppressing personal views to avoid conflict.

Key Types of Societal Pressure

- **Peer pressure:** Influence from friends or peers to conform to their behaviours and beliefs is commonly observed in adolescent social circles.

- **Academic pressure:** Stress is associated with achieving high grades, meeting academic expectations, and competing with peers in a school environment.

- **Family pressure:** Expectations and influences imposed on individuals by family members regarding career choices, life partners, or personal values.

- **Social media pressure:** The effect of social media platforms on individuals' self-image often promotes unrealistic beauty standards and lifestyle representations.

- **Conformity pressure:** The fear of social rejection drives the inclination to adjust one's behavior or opinions to match the majority within a group.

- **Cultural pressure:** Cultural norms and expectations influence an individual's behavior and decisions.

- **Economic pressure:** Pressure related to financial stability, career advancement, and societal expectations around wealth.

- **Gender pressure:** Societal expectations regarding gender roles and behaviours impact individuals' choices and self-perception.

Important Points to Remember about Societal Pressure

- **Positive aspects:** Societal pressure can sometimes motivate individuals to strive for personal improvement or contribute positively to their community.

- **Negative Impacts:** Excessive societal pressure can result in stress, anxiety, low self-esteem, and unhealthy coping mechanisms.

- **Individual Variations:** People react to societal pressure differently depending on their personality, social group, and cultural background.

Key Aspects of How Societal Pressure Affects Individuals

- **Conformity:** A primary effect is the tendency to conform to group norms and expectations, even when they conflict with personal beliefs, to avoid social rejection or disapproval.

- **Self-Esteem Issues:** When individuals feel compelled to meet unrealistic standards, it can lead to feelings of inadequacy, low self-worth, and concerns about body image, particularly regarding beauty norms.

- **Decision-Making:** Societal pressure can influence decision-making by prompting individuals to prioritize what is considered “socially acceptable” over their desires, resulting in choices they may later regret.

- **Stress and Anxiety**: The continuous pressure to conform can lead to increased stress and anxiety, especially when individuals sense they are not meeting societal expectations.

- **Identity Struggles:** Individuals might struggle to cultivate a strong sense of self if they constantly attempt to fit into societal molds, which can confuse their values and aspirations.

Examples of Societal Pressure in Action

Appearance-Based Pressure:

- Feeling obligated to maintain a specific body type or dress in a particular way to be deemed attractive.

- **Career Expectations**: Feeling pressured to pursue a lucrative job or a specific career path due to social norms.

- **Academic Pressure:** Students experience tremendous pressure to achieve high grades to meet societal expectations of academic success.

- **Social Media Influence:** Feeling the need to present an ideal life online to conform to social media standards.

How to Manage Societal Pressure:

- **Self-Awareness:** Acknowledging the societal pressures, you encounter and understanding their effects on your choices.

Developing Strong Personal Values:

Having a clear understanding of what is important to you and feeling confident in upholding those values, even if they differ from societal norms.

- **Building a Supportive Network:** Surround yourself with individuals who accept and support your uniqueness.
- **Setting Healthy Boundaries:** Learning to decline things that make you uncomfortable or contradict your values.
- **Seeking Professional Help:** If societal pressure significantly affects your mental health, consider seeking therapy to develop coping strategies.

Embracing individualism involves recognizing and valuing one's unique qualities and life path and resisting the urge to conform to unrealistic societal standards.

About the Author

Emmanuel Victor Opasola popularly called *Apostle of Love* is a Nigerian clergy whose vision is to herald apostolic existence in the body of Christ at large. He believes that we are in the last days and the present day church must return to the ways of the early church. He seeks to see a rise of young men like himself who share the burden of the rebirth of the first apostolic cultures.

He has an apostolic community in Nigeria where communal lifestyle as in the early church is being practiced. He is a conservative and upholds the belief that Christians must live in moderation because the coming of the Lord is near.

Chapter 2

RITUAL SYMBOLISM

Understanding the symbolism in Religious Rituals

Rituals form the foundation of many religious traditions, expressing beliefs, values, and the profound mysteries of life and the divine. These rituals are often rich in symbolism, employing actions, objects, and language to convey complex meanings that resonate deeply with practitioners.

This writing explores the concept of ritual symbolism, examining its significance, cultural variations, and role in fostering community, expressing the sacred, and bridging the tangible and intangible.

The Nature of Ritual Symbolism

Symbols play a crucial role in human communication, representing ideas or concepts that extend beyond their literal meanings. In religious rituals, symbols connect the physical world with spiritual or metaphysical realms. A ritual is a set of prescribed actions performed in a specific sequence, often carrying a symbolic meaning that transcends the immediate act.

For example, lighting a candle during prayer can symbolize enlightenment, the presence of the divine, or the purification of the soul. Similarly, kneeling during worship may signify humility, submission, or reverence. These physical gestures and objects hold meanings specific to particular religious traditions but can also possess universal significance, tapping into shared human experiences and archetypes.

Functions of Ritual Symbolism

Ritual symbolism serves various functions within religious and cultural contexts. Some of its primary purposes include:

1. **Conveying the Sacred:**
   Rituals transform everyday spaces, objects, and actions into expressions of the sacred. Through symbolism, practitioners engage with the divine in ways that stimulate the senses and evoke emotions. For example, in the Christian tradition, the Eucharist employs bread and wine as symbols of the body and blood of Christ, turning a simple meal into a profound spiritual experience.

2. **Expressing Community and Identity:**
   Rituals frequently use symbols to reinforce group identity and shared beliefs. For instance, the Jewish Passover Seder includes symbolic foods such as bitter herbs to remember ancestors' suffering, enhancing a sense of collective memory and unity.

3. **Bridging the Seen and Unseen**: Symbols in rituals often serve as intermediaries between the physical and spiritual worlds. Smoke from incense, for instance, is seen in many traditions as carrying prayers to the heavens, visually representing the ascent of human intention to the divine realm.

4. **Marking Transitions**: Many rituals, such as weddings, funerals, or rites of passage, symbolize transitions in life stages. In Hindu weddings, tying the "mangalsutra" (sacred thread) represents the bond between husband and wife, a visible marker of a new phase in their lives.

5. **Teaching and Preserving Doctrine**: Rituals encode and transmit religious teachings and values through symbolic elements. The Islamic practice of Salah (prayer) includes gestures and recitations that reflect submission to God and unity among believers, reinforcing key tenets of faith.

Symbolism in Rituals across Religions

Religious traditions worldwide employ an array of symbols within their rituals. While the meanings may vary, specific themes recur, reflecting universal human concerns such as life, death, renewal, and connection to the divine.

Christianity

In Christianity, rituals such as baptism and communion are deeply symbolic. Baptism, involving water, signifies purification, rebirth, and initiation into the faith. The immersion or sprinkling of water represents the washing away of sin and the beginning of a new spiritual life.

The Eucharist, or Holy Communion, is another central ritual laden with symbolism. Bread and wine are consecrated to become the body and blood of Christ, recalling the Last Supper and Jesus's sacrificial death. This ritual commemorates Christ's sacrifice and fosters a sense of spiritual nourishment and unity among believers.

Hinduism

Hindu rituals are replete with symbolism, often tied to cosmic principles and the divine. The use of fire in "yajna" (sacrificial rituals) symbolizes purification and the presence of Agni, the fire deity who acts as a messenger between humans and gods. Offerings made into the fire are believed to reach the deities, emphasizing the reciprocal relationship between the divine and the devotee.

Another prominent symbol in Hindu rituals is the lotus flower, representing purity, spiritual awakening, and divine beauty. It is often used in worship and offerings, reflecting the ideal of rising above worldly impurities to attain spiritual enlightenment.

Islam

Islamic rituals emphasize submission to God (Allah) and the unity of the faithful. The five daily prayers (Salah) include physical movements such as bowing and prostration, symbolizing humility and devotion. The direction of prayer toward the Kaaba in Mecca signifies the unity of Muslims worldwide in worshiping one God.

During the Hajj pilgrimage, rituals such as the Tawaf (circumambulation of the Kaaba) and the stoning of the pillars at Mina carry profound symbolic meanings. Tawaf represents the unity of believers as they move in harmony around the central symbol of God's presence. At the same time, the stoning of the pillars symbolizes the rejection of evil and temptation.

Buddhism

Buddhist rituals often use symbols to convey teachings and aid meditation. The mandala, a geometric design used in rituals and meditation, symbolizes the universe and the path to enlightenment. Its intricate patterns guide the practitioner's focus, illustrating the impermanence and interconnectedness of all things.

Another common symbol in Buddhist rituals is offering a lit lamp or candle, signifying the dispelling of ignorance and the attainment of wisdom. Similarly, bells ringing during ceremonies represent clarity and the call to mindfulness.

A. Indigenous and Animistic Traditions

Indigenous and animistic traditions worldwide incorporate symbols that reflect a deep connection to nature and ancestral spirits. In Native American rituals, the eagle feather symbolizes strength, freedom, and a connection to the spiritual realm. Using the sacred pipe in ceremonies represents the harmony between humans, nature, and the Creator.

In African traditional religions, rituals often involve symbols such as masks and drums. Masks worn during ceremonies are believed to channel ancestral spirits or deities, allowing participants to interact with the spiritual world. On the other hand, drumming symbolizes communication with the divine and the rhythm of life itself.

B. Interpretation and Variability of Symbolism

While symbols within rituals carry profound meanings, their interpretation can vary widely depending on cultural, historical, and individual contexts. A single symbol may evoke different emotions and associations among practitioners. For instance, water in rituals can symbolize life, purification, destruction, or transformation, depending on the tradition and context.

Moreover, the meanings of symbols can evolve. Practices once tied to specific historical or cultural circumstances may take on new interpretations in different eras or communities. For example, the Christian cross, initially a symbol of suffering and execution, has come to represent redemption and hope.

C. Psychological and Sociological Perspectives

Ritual symbolism also has significant psychological and sociological dimensions. Carl Jung, the renowned psychoanalyst, viewed symbols as expressions of the collective unconscious, containing archetypal meanings that resonate across cultures. Through their symbols, rituals allow individuals to connect with these more profound layers of the psyche, fostering personal and communal integration.

From a sociological perspective, ritual symbols help maintain social cohesion and reinforce shared values. Emile Durkheim, a foundational figure in sociology, argued that rituals and their symbols affirm the collective identity of a community, strengthening bonds among its members. This function is evident in rituals like national anthems, which use symbols of unity to evoke patriotism and collective pride.

D. **Challenges in Understanding Ritual Symbolism**

While ritual symbolism is significant, it can also be challenging to interpret, particularly for those outside a tradition. Symbols often rely on a shared cultural and historical framework, which may not be immediately accessible to outsiders. Misinterpretations can lead to misunderstandings or the diminishment of a ritual's significance.

Additionally, in increasingly secular and pluralistic societies, the symbolic aspects of rituals may lose their resonance for some individuals. Symbols that once held profound meaning may be reduced to mere tradition or spectacle, disconnected from their original context and purpose.

E. The Future of Ritual Symbolism

As societies evolve, so too does the role and interpretation of ritual symbolism. Globalization and interfaith interactions have led to a blending and reimagining of rituals and their symbols. While this can enrich traditions, it raises questions about authenticity and cultural appropriation.

At the same time, there is a renewed interest in rituals and their symbols as tools for personal and communal transformation. Practices such as mindfulness meditation, often adapted from Buddhist rituals, use symbols like the breath or a mantra to foster inner peace and self-awareness. Similarly, environmental movements have adopted rituals incorporating natural symbols, emphasizing humanity's interconnectedness with the earth.

Conclusion

Ritual symbolism lies at the heart of religious practice, providing a powerful means of expressing the sacred, fostering community, and connecting the physical and spiritual realms. Rituals communicate complex ideas and evoke profound emotional and spiritual responses through gestures, objects, and actions imbued with symbolic meaning.

While the interpretation of symbols may vary across cultures and contexts, their universal themes reflect shared human concerns and aspirations. As the world continues to change, the enduring power of ritual symbolism reminds us of our deep-seated need for meaning, connection, and transcendence. Whether through ancient rites or modern adaptations, these symbols speak to the human spirit, bridging the gap between the seen and unseen, the temporal and the eternal.

About the Author

Olutunu Babalola-Daniel encountered God as a committed Christian 37 years ago. She is an intercessor, a teacher of the word, and a worshiper.

Over the years, Olutunu has assisted and pioneered church planting projects and worked as a bible-study teacher, youth leader, church administrator, treasurer, and trustee. Olutunu is passionate about pulling down strongholds and seeing captives set free from Satan's Kingdom through intense prayers. *'The Arsenal of the Christian'* is Olutunu's first writing project. In this book, she has used her life experiences to explore all the weapons the Lord has equipped every believer with for living a spirit-filled and purposeful life.

Olutunu currently attends *RCCG Impact Centre Church* in Bicester. She is married to Rotimi Patrick Daniel.

CHAPTER 3

TOGETHER AND MORE

A Short Reflection

"Father, please help me decrease in my life so You can increase. I'm making a mess of it."

"What do you mean, son?"

"You know, Lord, like John the Baptist said. I need to dwindle to nothing and for You to become everything in my life, so that the people I meet only ever see Jesus."

"Whoa there! You know I love you, but you've got that so, so wrong. If I had a gram of Gold for every time I hear that misinterpretation, I'd be wealthy. (Only joking, the whole universe is Mine!)"

"But what then, Father? What did John mean, and what should I think now?"

"There are several parts to this, so walk me through it. It isn't difficult. What my friend John the Baptist meant was that His God-given time in the spotlight had come to an end, as My herald to prepare people for Jesus's coming, and now it was time for John to step back and pretty much just point people to Jesus, encouraging them to grab hold of what He was doing and saying."

"OK. What's the other bit? What would you most like me to do, 'cos I'm grateful to you for all you have done and do in my life in so many wonderful ways. What can I do to delight you, Father?"

"Oh, bless you, son - I love it when your heart says things like that. But listen carefully now. It's not about what I want you to do, it's about what I want us to be, together."

"I'm confused. Please would you unpack that for me, (which I guess you already knew I was going to ask!)"

"Got it in one. You thought I wanted you to diminish, as if I wanted to make a takeover bid to occupy all your life, and nobody sees the real you anymore. Ha! Nothing could be further from the truth! Yes, of course, I want you to stop making bad choices, as if you are still on the throne of your life and messing everything up, because you told me I could do a much better job of it. (An understatement, of course!) And I took you seriously. But that's not the best bit!

"Go on, please, Father; You've got my attention now."

"I never wanted you to diminish. I have always wanted the real, amazingly unique you to become more evident, polished up, and wonderfully obvious. If you pause and think for a moment, you'll see that those you know who are walking most closely with Me are, (in the very best and richest sense), gloriously eccentric! And I love it!

"Oh yes! I hadn't noticed that, but now you mention it, I can see it's true! The world, living without reference to You, wants us to conform, to be "different like everybody else", but You are saying that You celebrate how each of us is, truly, different. No beige and drab lives in Your Kingdom! Is that about right, Father?"

"Exactly. I have never done "One size fits all" or asked my people to become any less wonderfully individual than they truly are. It made me cry when Mao Zedong got his millions in China, and all of them dressed alike in identical drab uniforms. Let their individuality shine!"

"OK, I think I might begin seeing what you're getting at. Can we now please go back to what you said about not being about what I do, but rather being about what you want us to be, together?"

"Of course. This is where I've been leading you throughout this conversation. You thought I wanted you to empty yourself, diminishing to nothing. That's not it at all. Here's what I want, (yes, I did inspire those song words – I love it when praying people get to the point), I want all of you to be in me, and me to be in all of you, a life shared! And then we'll make the real you shine, and other people can truly enjoy meeting the richness of us both. THAT's what I'm talking about!"

"I am almost speechless, Loving Father. Your ways, your character, your purposes, are truly awesome."

"Love you, Son. Let's walk and talk some more, anytime you like. I love spending time with my friends."

I have always wanted the real, amazingly unique you to become more evident, polished up, and wonderfully obvious.

About the Author

Tim Simpson's story is a powerful testament to God's sovereignty and love. In 1966, at just 15 years old, Tim's life was dramatically changed when God convicted him of sin and revealed His love in a profound way. Without any prior Christian background, Tim was suddenly and irreversibly drawn into God's Kingdom.

His encounter was marked by intense conviction, desperate prayer, and an overwhelming sense of forgiveness. From that moment on, Tim's life was forever changed, and he began a journey of deepening his relationship with God. His story highlights the transformative power of God's grace and the importance of personal faith.

CHAPTER 4

READING HUMAN BEHAVIOUR

If you can read the underlying causes of a friend's behaviour instead of judging them superficially.

> *"To understand is to forgive. When you truly understand the struggles, fears, and motivations behind someone's actions, judgment dissolves, and compassion takes its place."*
>
> – Unknown

At some point, we have all faced moments where we felt misunderstood or judged. Perhaps it was during a personal struggle when our actions didn't align with others' expectations or when fear clouded our decisions. In those moments, we experienced what appeared to be unfair judgment from those around us. We felt misunderstood, and to an even greater extent, we felt unloved. The judgment of others felt heavy, isolating, and unfair. It left us confused and alone! And yet, having been through these hurtful experiences, we fail to put others in our shoes when we unfairly judge them for their behaviour.

Judith had been planning her 40th birthday for 2 years; every day, she prayed as she counted the days in excitement. Her 40th birthday was supposed to be the perfect celebration—a day she would remember for years. She wanted her day filled with joy and laughter, and for everyone to have a special place in her life. Her closest friend Faith had been the driving force behind the event's planning. From helping her choose the venue and theme to putting together the guest list and finalizing the details, she was there for every decision. Faith knew how much this milestone meant to Judith, and Judith was excited to celebrate not just the day but the prayers and friendship that made it all possible.

On the evening of the party, everything was in place. The decorations were perfect, the music was playing, and the room was filled with the people Judith loved the most. But as the hours passed, Judith greeted guests with hugs and smiles. She soon realised that Faith was nowhere to be found! She couldn't help but notice her absence. At first, she told herself she was running late—maybe stuck in traffic or dealing with a last-minute hiccup. She kept looking at the door, waiting to see her walk in with her usual smile and the infectious energy she always brought. The party was in full swing, and so were the whispers and questions. Is Faith ok? Where is Faith? Is there any reason she's not here?

As reality began to sink in, Judith felt a growing knot in her stomach. She tried to hide it behind laughter and polite conversations, but internally, she was in turmoil. A part of her couldn't focus on what was supposed to be the best day of her life. She called Faith's phone over 50 times, but all 50 times, the phone went to voicemail. Judith was left battling a whirlwind of emotions—anger at her for letting her down, sadness because her absence stung more than she cared to admit, and a deep sense of rejection that she couldn't shake. She needed Faith there. She wasn't just any friend; she was supposed to be standing right next to Judith, making this milestone unforgettable.

"Surely it's time to get new friends!" Sharon said with a chuckle. "I could never accept such behaviour. Maybe Faith is jealous that you've got the spotlight and not her. I've never really believed she was a good friend," she said as a matter of fact.

The words stung Judith, but inwardly, she couldn't help but wonder if there was truth to what Sharon had said. She held back tears threatening to spill out on her perfectly contoured cheeks. She smiled for pictures, clinked glasses, and danced with guests, trying to enjoy the party she had worked so hard to plan. But every moment felt incomplete. Every time she looked around the room, she was reminded of the space where she should have been. It was a shadow she couldn't escape, and she found myself replaying everything in my head—why didn't she tell me? How could she miss something so important?

Judith's concern and confusion from the previous night turned to anger and rejection the next day. When she woke up, she had decided never to speak to Faith again. Judith could not bring herself to attend Church that morning. Her heart was filled with pain and slight hatred for someone she had previously cared for. Two decades of friendship suddenly ended in one night. Sharon was right; she deserved better friends!

"How could she do this to me? Judith asked herself over and over again. "The one person I have counted on all these years! How could she do this to me?"

The sound of the mobile phone vibrating jolted Judith. She rushed to answer the phone. It was Faith's brother Jack on the phone. Hatred and anger rose within her. She hesitated to answer the phone, wondering to herself why Jack was calling her. What poor excuse did his sister come up with? She was not going to be made a fool by either of them. Judith ignored the call.

Later that afternoon, Judith heard an unexpected knock at her door. When she opened it, there stood Faith, looking drained and utterly exhausted. Without a moment's hesitation, Judith's emotions boiled over. She screamed in Faith's face, her anger pouring out in unfiltered words. "Leave!" Judith shouted. Her hurt and disappointment were palpable. Faith broke down in tears right there on the doorstep. She looked fragile, her body trembling as she sobbed uncontrollably. "Judith, I'm sorry," she muttered between gasping sobs. "I'm so sorry. Please, I need to speak with you."

Judith hesitated, her anger battling the deep bond of friendship they had shared for years. Seeing Faith in tears softened her resolve. With a heavy sigh, she stepped aside and let Faith in. "You have five minutes, and then I want you gone," Judith said coldly. Whatever excuse you have, make it quick."

Faith reached into her bag and handed Judith a folded document. It was a hospital discharge note. As Judith read it, her legs buckled, and she sank to her knees. The words blurred as tears welled up in her eyes. Miscarriage. Faith had been through a miscarriage on the day of Judith's birthday.

Realisation hit her like a giant wave. Guilt and sadness engulfed her, washing away the anger she had clung to moments earlier. Judith began to sob uncontrollably, her heart breaking for her friend. "I'm so sorry, Faith. I didn't know. I didn't understand," she said over and over.

Faith's voice trembled as she explained. "I didn't want to ruin your birthday, Judith. I could handle it, but I just couldn't."

The weight of her friend's pain crushed Judith's spirit. She reached out, pulling Faith into a tight embrace, their tears mingling as they held each other. At that moment, Judith realized that their friendship was worth fighting for, even in her anger and hurt, and forgiveness became the only path forward.

What we learn from this story is a valuable lesson on perspective and compassion. Life comes with ups and downs; sometimes, the people we love and care for let us down, not because they don't love us, but because they're fighting battles we can't see. While Judith felt justified to feel hurt, rejected, disappointed, sad, and angry, she realized that friendships, like life, are about navigating the messy, complicated moments with grace. Faith wasn't there that night, but their bond was strong enough to weather it. The story further reminds us to have compassion; we must always leave room for compassion amid negative emotions. When we take time to see the struggles, fears, and motivations behind someone's actions, we replace judgment with empathy. It's a powerful shift that fosters trust, strengthens relationships, and allows us to become kinder, more supportive versions of ourselves.

Understanding human behaviour is not easy; it requires a heart rooted in empathy and compassion. A heart like our Lord Jesus Christ. When we look at the life of Jesus, we see how He looked beyond surface actions and saw the deeper motivations. When Judas betrayed him, all Jesus felt was compassion and love. According to scripture, *"Jesus asked him, 'Friend, do you betray the Son of Man with a kiss?'"* (**Luke 22:48**). Notice how Jesus still calls Judas "friend" even in moments of betrayal. Another scripture that shows us the compassion Christ had is found in Luke 23:34. He said, "Father, forgive them, for they do not know what they are doing," showing ultimate compassion for those who wronged Him:

When faced with what appears to be hurtful actions from friends or family, instead of jumping to judgment, pausing to read the underlying causes of their behaviour fosters compassion and understanding. (**Proverbs 20:5**) reminds us, *"The purposes of a person's heart are deep waters, but one who has insight draws them out."* This wisdom teaches us to approach others with patience and care, seeking to uncover the intentions and emotions that shape their actions. By doing so, we strengthen our relationships and reflect the grace and mercy God extends to us daily.

When faced with what appears to be hurtful actions from friends or family, instead of jumping to judgment, pausing to read the underlying causes of their behaviour fosters compassion and understanding.

About the Author

Bubles Nekatambe is a seasoned Career Consultant and Director of *Career Consulting & Solutions Ltd.* With more than 8 years of experience, she empowers individuals to discover their purpose and achieve career success. Her client-focused approach has helped hundreds gain clarity and confidence.

Bubles is committed to social impact, supporting vulnerable communities through *Good Hope Mothers.* Guided by biblical values, she integrates faith into her work, believing success comes from walking in alignment with God's plan. With purpose, empathy, and faith, Bubles serves others, whether through her career work or community involvement, inspiring others with her dedication and compassion.

CHAPTER 5

FAMILY DYNAMICS EFFECT

Recognizing the influences of family dynamics on personal development.

A family plays a crucial role in the development of everyone involved. It can be defined as a group of people living together and sharing the same DNA. However, an 'ideal family' is marked by love, support, communication, and trust, which foster a healthy family dynamic. But what are family dynamics? Family dynamics refer to the connections, interactions, exchanges, and relationships formed through trust, love, and communication. More formally, they can be defined as 'patterns of interactions and relationships within a family, which include how members communicate, make decisions, and show affection.' Christian families must engage in daily worship and family time to nurture a dynamic family.

How Does Being Christian Relate To Family?

Firstly, the Lord God believes in family. Genesis 2:15 states that the Lord God gave Adam and Eve the Garden of Eden and granted Adam dominion over everything. This is one of the reasons He created Adam and Eve as the first family.

Secondly, **Ephesians 5:25** states, *'For husbands, this means love your wives, just as Christ loved the church.'* In **Ephesians 5:22,** wives are instructed to submit to their husbands as to the Lord. This demonstrates the Lord's emphasis on families, highlighting the necessity *of love and respect between partners within the household.*

In Jeremiah 1:5, God says, 'Before I formed you in the womb, I knew you; before you were born, I set you apart.' To be 'set apart' indicates that God loves His children and is prepared to care for them. This is God's declaration that we are all unique, regardless of age or gender.

Parents who work closely with their children during their formative years help to guide them into adulthood. **Proverbs 22:6** says, *'Train up a child in the way he should go; even when he is old, he will not depart from it.'* This further reinforces the importance of guiding children well. Parents must ensure they share positive ideas and values rooted in the word of God because children are 'sponges,' meaning they **are receptive to learning.** Remember the ideas, discussions, and decisions shared with them, shaping who they become.

Respect In the Household

The household must cultivate a high level of respect. 1 Peter 2:17 states, 'Show proper respect to everyone, love the family of believers. Fear God, honour the emperor.' Respect should not be merely given but must be earned correctly, which involves fearing God and honouring Him in spirit and truth. Respect takes many forms: a simple thank you (acknowledgment for a kind deed or work), treating others how you wish to be treated, actively listening to each other, and demonstrating loyalty. Everyone should be able to recognize qualities that enhance each other's lives.

Parents should commend their children for their outstanding qualities and address traits that may negatively affect their mindset. They must remember that their role is to guide and serve as role models. By modelling respect, parents are, in essence, teaching their children to reciprocate, allowing them to understand and learn from their mistakes.

Trust In the Household

A healthy household dynamic encourages members to be considerate and respectful of each other's feelings. Parents occasionally overlook their children's emotions, which may make them feel that their opinions and thoughts are not valued. This approach undermines trust-building efforts.

Raising children should never be a power struggle, especially when God is at the center of everything. The focus should be on understanding and love, enabling everyone involved to express I am sorry, I understand, I recognize the error, so let's talk about it. While this may be challenging, it's not impossible. **Luke 18:27** illustrates God's power in every situation; *'The things which are impossible with men are possible with God.'*

In a family with strong dynamics, high levels of trust are vital. What is trust? You must believe in their reliability, honesty, and effectiveness to trust someone. Most of us go to bed with plans for the next day, trusting God to wake us up. **Proverbs 29:25** states,'...whoever trusts in the Lord is kept safe.' Because we trust in the Lord, we plan for the following day. For weeks and even months. This is with the expectation that we will wake up and proceed with all our plans. As children of God, we feel confident and safe knowing that God can do what he said he would do.

To cultivate a high level of trust, trust must first be established within a family. Establishing trust takes time. Trust is first established between parents, which is then extended to the children. To be trustworthy, you must be reliable, have integrity, and feel safe within the relationship.

'Broken promises mean broken trust.' Parents must strive to be committed and show that they are not afraid of making mistakes, allowing their children to understand that no one is perfect, and mistakes can be made. This approach should empower children to develop a better mindset towards challenges and life. **Philippians 4:13** says, *'I can* *do all things through Christ who strengthens me.'* As children of God, we should understand that without Christ, we are nothing, and all things are only possible with Christ. As Christians, it is essential to have daily worship as a family. It should be the time for bonding as a family unit.

Ephesians 3:20 says, *'God is able to do exceedingly, abundantly, above all we ask or think.'* Whatever we desire of the Lord, he will make it a reality. Children and young adults might find this difficult to understand, but parents must point out God's work's realities by sharing their testimonies. If children can recognize the work of God in their parents, it becomes more relatable to them.

Love in the Household

Love is a lynchpin in helping foster strong family dynamics. **John 3:16**, a well-known scripture, says, *'For God so loved the world, that he gave his only begotten Son, that whosoever believeth in him should not perish, but have everlasting life.'* Everyone needs love, especially children. Children generally feel loved when interacting with their parents in a conflict-free environment. By providing children with love, they will form their boundaries, allowing them to reflect and grow.

Parents should do their best to understand their children, both young and old. They can ask questions like: How was your day? How are you feeling today? Offering hugs and expressing love are essential, too. These actions will help parents learn more about their children's strengths and weaknesses and foster a stronger sense of family. In the family structure, everyone will have their own experiences throughout the day and may need a shoulder to lean on.

The more a family unites, the more they work as a team, showing and embracing love, and strong bonding will develop. This means that family members will feel comfortable sharing issues that they might be experiencing. Their more profound innermost thoughts and feelings might be expressed to parents, who will likely be their confidants and good friends. Our love for each other must be evident just as God's love for us. **Psalm 107:8-7** says, *'God's love is unfailing, and he satisfies the thirsty and fills the hungry.'* God never fails us, and his love is everlasting. It might seem sometimes impossible to fully embrace what God wants for us as his children and how effectively we can live through Christ as families and individuals.

Communication in the Family

Communication is key to further developing a strong, dynamic family. Communication in the household involves having open dialogues and conversations to ensure everyone feels safe and connected. Parents must be active listeners, be attentive, ask questions, and be encouraging and supportive during discussions. **James 1:19** states Understand this*, my dear brothers and sisters, you must all be quick to listen, slow to speak, and slow to get angry.'* This verse underpins the idea of how you should control your emotions and think before you speak. One should be more conscious of what to say since information can be received negatively or positively depending on the tone and other factors**. Colossians 4:6** states, *'Let your conversation be always full of grace, seasoned with salt, so you may know how to answer everyone.'*

We are not perfect; all we need as a family is to make that effort and try. Family needs to show love, communicate well, and trust each other. With these factors in place, a better generation will emerge, as they will know who they are and have experienced the nearness of God.

A healthy household dynamic encourages members to be considerate and respectful of each other's feelings.

About the Author

Joan A. Green, MA in Education, has been teaching since 1988. A devoted follower of Christ, she inspires young minds to stay rooted in faith through her ministry. Married and a mother of four, she has also embraced many through teaching. Joan is the author of '*The Power of Working With Your Child'* and Amazon bestseller *'All You Need to Know About 11+'*, which has helped dozens of children gain places in UK grammar schools.

Through workshops and online events, she equips parents with strategies to support their children's learning without pressure. Her guides stem from the success of these events and the growing need to motivate students returning to school with unfinished homework.

CHAPTER 6

ENLIST

A Short Conversation

"Father, as I wait here to receive this bread and wine in memory of Your death, I am acutely aware of my sins, how I fall so far short of Your standards, how I choose the wrong path again and again, how I go my way repeatedly. Lord, I am so weak and unworthy, and..."

"Shut up! I love you, not what you do or don't do."

"Huh?"

"Stop going on about your sins. Thank you. I don't need you to catalogue them for me this way. Do you think that's what I'm interested in, wanting to hear a list of your failures?"

"Well, I suppose not, but I know you want me to live rightly, and I mess up so often, and..."

"Enough! You don't notice what you're doing. You're making it all about you. About your failures, you willfully choose the bad. That's not the way to change anything for the better. Look at Me."

"Yes, Father."

"When you look at me, do you see your sins, or my goodness? Do you see me sitting down with my face in my hands, despairing of you, or do you see me standing, looking for you, waiting for your return in repentance, with my arms wide open in acceptance?"

"You mean you're not angry with me for my sin?"

"Oh no, son, but that is what many people think. Listen! I am with you against your sin. That's what my crucifixion was all about! Sin spoils your life and others, and I'm on your side, cheering you on every time you turn away from temptations, selfish choices, and towards the good stuff. As you turn away from it, I'm helping you take the following steps."

"Really? That's amazing."

"You are still very young in your understanding of Me, son, but as we share your life daily, we're getting there, one small step at a time! Do you remember what my friend Paul wrote to My people living in Philippi, (in what you call chapter 4), after he told them not to worry and to talk to Me instead, and just after the bit about how that would release My peace to stand guard over their hearts and minds as they rest in Me?"

"Um, I'm sure I've read it, Father, but now I confess I don't remember. What was it, please?"

"OK, here it is, and this is one way to help you forget your failings and deliberate sins. I prompted Paul to encourage them to fix their minds on all the good stuff, not the bad. Instead of fretting about the darkness, open your mind to My glorious truths, open the curtains, and embrace My light. Welcome My Presence; relish My love, mercy, and forgiveness. As another friend wrote, *'My Presence is fullness of joy'*, and that's what I want for you, son!"

"Wow, Lord! Your loving kindness towards me blows my mind again and again. And I have messed up so much over the years. That old hymn talks about *'Onward Christian soldiers...'* but I have lost far more battles than I've won!"

"There you go again. I do not sit and keep a catalogue of such things for my children. I am more interested in cheering you on whenever you take even one small step in the right direction, in the way of love, kindness, and gratefully serving others with me. Now, Son, listen carefully."

"Yes, Father, I'm listening."

"This is how another of my friends recorded my thought: On that day, the question will not be about how many battles you won or lost, but about on which side you enlist and fight, and from heaven's perspective, the answer is clear. I know you're on my team, and I love it!"

I'm on your side,
cheering you on every
time you turn away
from temptations,
selfish choices, and
towards the good stuff.

About the Author

Tim Simpson's story is a powerful testament to God's sovereignty and love. In 1966, at just 15 years old, Tim's life was dramatically changed when God convicted him of sin and revealed His love in a profound way. Without any prior christian background, Tim was suddenly and irreversibly drawn into God's Kingdom.

His encounter was marked by intense conviction, desperate prayer, and an overwhelming sense of forgiveness. From that moment on, Tim's life was forever changed, and he began a journey of deepening his relationship with God. His story highlights the transformative power of God's grace and the importance of personal faith.

CHAPTER 7

FASHION AS A CULTURAL BAROMETER

Recognising how Fashion Trends reflect Societal Values

Fashion is far more than a fleeting trend or a mere aesthetic pursuit. It acts as a cultural barometer, reflecting society's values, ideologies, and aspirations at any given moment. Throughout history, clothing has been used for self-expression and as a mirror that showcases the time's political, social, and economic climates. By examining fashion trends, we gain a unique insight into the collective psyche of cultures, revealing how identity, innovation, and change are expressed through dress.

Fashion's Historical Ties to Society

Early Civilizations: Clothing as Status and Ritual
In early societies, clothing often went beyond its practical use to become a marker of status, identity, and spirituality. In ancient Egypt, delicate linen garments adorned with intricate jewellery symbolised wealth, power, and divine favour. Similarly, in medieval Europe, sumptuary laws dictated who could wear specific colours and fabrics, ensuring that fashion remained a clear signifier of social rank.

Clothing also played an essential role in rituals and traditions. In indigenous cultures, ceremonial attire made of feathers, beads, or animal hides often conveyed spiritual significance, highlighting the profound interplay between fashion and cultural values.

The Renaissance: Individualism and Artistry

The Renaissance marked a dramatic shift toward individualism, a value vividly reflected in the time's fashion. Richly decorated fabrics, elaborate embroidery, and dramatic silhouettes became tools for personal expression.

Wealthy patrons used clothing to communicate status and sophistication, while the flourishing of art and culture was mirrored in bold colours and intricate designs. This era underscored how shifts in intellectual and cultural thought could reshape fashion.

Fashion as a Reflection of Societal Change

The Industrial Revolution: Democratization of Style

The Industrial Revolution transformed fashion by introducing mass production. With advancements in textile manufacturing and sewing machines, clothing became more affordable and accessible, breaking down barriers between social classes. This democratization of fashion aligned with the rise of the middle class and urbanization. Simultaneously, Victorian fashion reflected the moral values of the era. Restrictive corsets, high collars, and elaborate gowns symbolized modesty and propriety, while tailored suits for men emphasized discipline and industriousness. The convergence of technological innovation and societal norms shaped a distinctive aesthetic that encapsulated the spirit of the time.

The 20th Century: A Century of Revolution

The 20th century witnessed unprecedented societal shifts, with each decade leaving its mark on fashion:

The 1920s–*The Jazz Age*: The post-World War I era was characterized by liberation, shorter hemlines, loose silhouettes, and the rise of the flapper style. Women's fashion symbolised newfound freedom and defiance against Victorian constraints.

The 1930s–*The Great Depression:* Economic hardship influenced fashion, leading to more practical and durable clothing. Subdued colours and simpler designs mirrored a sombre societal mood.

The 1940s—Wartime Utility: Fabric rationing during World War II resulted in minimalist designs and utilitarian styles. Women's adoption of trousers showcased their expanding roles in the workforce.

The 1960s—*Countercultural Movements*: The rebellious spirit of the 1960s was embodied in vibrant colours, psychedelic prints, and unisex fashion. These trends reflected the era's fight for civil rights, gender equality, and anti-establishment values.

The 1980s–*The Age of Excess*: Power dressing, bold colours, and exaggerated silhouettes symbolized ambition, wealth, and individualism in a decade marked by materialism.

The 1990s—Minimalism and Grunge: In reaction to the excesses of the 1980s, the 1990s embraced simplicity and authenticity. Flannel shirts, slip dresses, and understated styles became defining features of this era.

Contemporary Fashion: Society in Flux

Sustainability and Ethical Practices

The growing awareness of environmental issues has made sustainability a key trend in modern fashion. Ethical consumption reflects society's values, leading to an increased demand for eco-friendly materials, transparent supply chains, and slow fashion. Brands prioritising sustainability resonate with consumers who value responsibility and long-term impact over fast, disposable trends.

Diversity And Representation

Modern fashion champions diversity and inclusivity more than ever. Runways and campaigns now feature models of all sizes, ages, ethnicities, and gender identities, challenging long-held beauty standards. This shift reflects a broader societal embrace of equality and a celebration of individual uniqueness. Designers like Prabal Gurung and Savage x Fenty by Rihanna have ensured that inclusivity is not just a trend but a core value of the fashion industry.

Global Influences

Fashion has increasingly embraced global influences, reflecting the interconnectedness of the modern world. Designers draw inspiration from traditional garments, textiles, and patterns, seamlessly blending them into contemporary creations. For example, Japanese streetwear's minimalist aesthetic and bold graphic designs have significantly impacted global trends. Similarly, African prints and textiles, such as Kente and Ankara, are being reimagined in modern contexts, often honouring the heritage and artistry of their origins. At the same time, the fusion of cultures in fashion has sparked essential discussions about cultural appropriation. While globalization has facilitated the exchange of ideas, it has also highlighted the importance of context and respect. This dynamic interplay between global and local identities ensures that fashion remains a vibrant and reflective art form.

Digital Innovation

The digital age has transformed the fashion landscape. Social media platforms like Instagram and TikTok set trends, enabling consumers to influence the industry in real-time. Virtual fashion and NFTs have arisen as new frontiers, showcasing society's embrace of technology and blending digital and physical realities. This shift highlights a desire for both innovation and accessibility in fashion. Furthermore, the emergence of digital influencers and virtual try-on technology has connected consumers with high fashion, making once-exclusive designs more available to a broader audience.

Fashion as a Medium for Advocacy

Political and Social Commentary

Clothing has long served as a tool for advocacy and protest. From the suffragettes' use of white dresses to symbolize purity and equality to the "Black Lives Matter" T-shirts worn during demonstrations, fashion is often at the forefront of social movements. Designers like Vivienne Westwood and brands like Patagonia utilize their platforms to address climate change, labour rights, and political unrest, demonstrating how fashion can inspire dialogue and action.

Addressing Cultural Appropriation
The global nature of the fashion industry has sparked discussions about cultural appropriation. Instances in which mainstream brands commodify traditional garments or symbols without context or credit have triggered calls for more respect and understanding. This discourse reflects a growing awareness of cultural heritage and the need to honour its significance.

The Future of Fashion as a Cultural Barometer

Looking forward, fashion will continue to evolve alongside societal values. Key trends likely to shape the future include:

Technological Advancements: Wearable tech, AI-driven design, and 3D printing are set to redefine the boundaries of fashion, reflecting society's increasing integration with technology.

Customisation and Personal Expression: Advances in manufacturing and digital tools will allow for hyper-personalization, enabling consumers to design garments that align with their unique identities.

Sustainability as Standard: As environmental awareness deepens, sustainable practices will become integral to the fashion industry's ethos, shaping design and consumer behaviour.

Global and Local Balance: While globalization promotes the exchange of ideas and aesthetics, there is a rising appreciation for local craftsmanship and traditional techniques, creating a dynamic interplay between global and regional influences.

Conclusion

Far from being superficial, fashion profoundly reflects society's values and transformations. From ancient symbols of status to today's sustainable, inclusive movements, it provides a window into the collective mindset of cultures across time. As technology, sustainability, and diversity continue to shape the industry, fashion remains an essential tool for understanding the ever-changing dynamics of human societies.

By examining fashion as a cultural barometer, we uncover its role as a storyteller that captures each generation's aspirations, challenges, and innovations. In doing so, fashion reflects who we are and helps shape who we strive to become.

Fashion has increasingly embraced global influences, reflecting the interconnectedness of the modern world.

About the Author

Olutunu Babalola-Daniel encountered God as a committed Christian 37 years ago. She is an intercessor, a teacher of the word, and a worshiper.

Over the years, Olutunu has assisted and pioneered church planting projects and worked as a bible-study teacher, youth leader, church administrator, treasurer, and trustee. Olutunu is passionate about pulling down strongholds and seeing captives set free from Satan's Kingdom through intense prayers. *'The Arsenal of the Christian'* is Olutunu's first writing project. In this book, she has used her life experiences to explore all the weapons the Lord has equipped every believer with for living a spirit-filled and purposeful life.

Olutunu currently attends *RCCG Impact Centre Church* in Bicester. She is married to Rotimi Patrick Daniel.

Chapter 8

MUSIC AS SOCIETY'S MIRROR

Recognising how Music reflects Societal Moods and Changes

Music often plays a key role in social events and religious ceremonies. Music-making techniques are typically transmitted as part of cultural traditions. Music is performed in public and private settings and showcased at festivals and concerts featuring various ensembles. It is used in producing other media, including soundtracks for films, TV shows, operas, and video games. Listening to music is a common form of entertainment. The culture surrounding music extends into academic study, journalism, philosophy, psychology, and therapy. The music industry encompasses songwriters, performers, sound engineers, producers, tour organizers, distributors of instruments and accessories, and publishers of sheet music and recordings. Technology that facilitates the recording and reproduction of music has historically included sheet music, microphones, phonographs, and tape machines, with the playback of digital music being a daily practice for MP3 players, CD players, and smartphones. Music as an agent for change is evident throughout history. One example is the impact of the "freedom songs" during the Civil Rights movement, such as "We Shall Overcome" and "Strange Fruit." These songs broke down barriers, educated people, fostered empathy across divides, and contributed to the end of segregation. Today, music continues to illuminate worldwide inequalities and will always act as an agent for change.

Given the profound influence of melodies and lyrics on society, we must know our current culture. More importantly, we must be mindful of the cultures we aspire to build and nurture through our music. Songs have the power to change the world in unforeseen ways, challenging preconceived notions and highlighting issues that have historically been overlooked. Our experiences show that music in schools enhances outcomes for students, teachers, and communities—and subsequently for society, particularly the future generation. Whether you're a music enthusiast or not, anyone can recognize music's impact on society. More than any other art form, music reflects society's constantly evolving emotional landscape. Over the years, artists have consistently utilized their music to create powerful dialogues with their audiences, and this connection has only deepened as societal values, struggles, and victories evolve. The way music mirrors society's emotional shifts extends beyond lyrics and melodies; it also encompasses the broader context in which it's created.

The music industry shapes the narrative by embracing new sounds, genres, and perspectives. Artists are no longer limited to a single genre or style; they can experiment, collaborate, and produce music that defies categorization. The rise of platforms like Spotify and Apple Music has further transformed this landscape.

- Music has democratized music consumption, allowing artists to gain exposure globally. This shift has allowed music to speak to broader audiences and capture various emotions, experiences, and cultural moments. The partnerships between record labels, streaming services, and independent artists are helping to amplify diverse voices, ensuring that music remains a powerful tool for social commentary.

- Music has shaped cultures and societies worldwide, passed down from generation to generation. It can alter one's mood, change perceptions, and inspire change. While everyone has a personal relationship with music, its effects on the culture around us may not be immediately apparent. Songs unify groups of people, move them to standard action, or help them express common emotions. Certain songs become "anthems" for generations, as Bob Dylan's "Blowin' in the Wind" (1962) became for many in the 1960s. In times of national crisis, certain songs seem especially appropriate, such as "God Bless America" or even John Lennon's "Imagine" (1971). They express shared values, experiences, and emotions that help define a group's identity and solidarity.

Songs, singers, and genres also help people construct self-images and provide models for how to behave. Pop stars–from Jenny Lind in the nineteenth century to Bing Crosby, Elvis Presley, and Britney Spears in the twentieth century–set styles and shape their fans' attitudes. They do this, moreover, in several ways. One is how the singer represents him or herself: Lind's charitable contributions, Bing's pipe, Elvis' ducktail haircut, and Britney's bare midriff. Genres such as punk rock or bebop provide fans with styles of dress, slang, and non-conformist identities. Naira Marley in Nigeria between 2019 and 2022 before the death of Mohbad (Imole) also dictated the hairstyles of the youths; they loved to be referred to as Martians back then, identifying with the Afro-Pop star, the death of one of his protege nicknamed Mohbad was the reason the flock of these youths rebelled against him, with the belief that he was involved with his demise.

Song lyrics also express judgments—and even conflicts—about lifestyles, values, and appearances. In the early 1970s, for example, Neil Young released two songs expressing anti-southern opinions: "Southern Man" (1970) and "Alabama" (1972). A few years later, a southern rock band, Lynard Skynard, responded with a defense of the South entitled "Sweet Home Alabama" (1974), containing the lines "I hope Neil Young will remember a southern man don't need him around, anyhow." Finally, music can express attitudes and values by how it sounds. Various popular forms like rock 'n roll and, beginning in the 1970s, such forms as punk, heavy metal, and rap sounded defiant, like an assault on the ears and the values of older generations. Historians sometimes consider songs as more or less straightforward "reflections" of the society and culture in which they were produced. These songs are then used to illustrate what historians already think they know about that society and culture. Thus, an anti-drinking song like "Come Home Father" (1864) might be interpreted to mean that nineteenth-century Americans were concerned about alcohol and opposed to its abuse. On one level, this view of music makes sense: a musical work is a product and a part of the society and culture from which it emerges. But such a view is also highly simplistic. It ignores the fact that songs exist about other popular texts, including other songs. "Come Home Father," for example, inspired a sequel by another composer, "Father Don't Drink any Now!" (1866), and both were part of the same musical universe as songs that treated drinking lightly, like "Pop, Pop, Pop. A Comic Song" (1868).

The assumption that songs merely reflect their times also ignores that songs are almost always open to multiple interpretations. For example, in the 1960s, "Puff the Magic Dragon" (1963) was widely associated with marijuana and its effects. Yet the lyricist, Leonard Lipton, claimed that the song was about the loss of childhood innocence. This interpretation prevailed because, by the 1970s, it had become standard repertoire at nursery schools and children's sing-alongs. The richness of using songs as sources for understanding history—and the need to delve deeply into the available evidence—lies in their openness to such multiple uses and interpretations.

However, multiple uses and interpretations point to another important aspect of music: it is a forum for public debate about manners, morals, politics, and social change. Musicians and their audiences are social actors; while they reflect the world around them, they also interpret and change it.

For every anti-Vietnam War song like "I-Feel-Like-I'm-Fix-in'-To-Die Rag" (1967), there were pro-war (or anti-anti-war) songs like "Ballad of the Green Berets" (1966). In cases like this, songs are invaluable for revealing what concerned individuals, how they perceived issues, and articulating their hopes, ideals, anger, and frustrations. Many historians have utilized song lyrics to better understand the culture and consciousness of the people who created and engaged with them. This is particularly significant for communities that left few written records of their lives, as song lyrics can provide crucial insights into what people thought and felt, their everyday struggles, and their aspirations for the future.

- Music also plays a vital role in politics. Politics is a sensitive subject that many people in prominent positions, such as celebrities and major artists, may hesitate to discuss due to fears of negative public backlash that could impact their popularity or income. Music offers artists a platform to express their political views and educate audiences about current global issues. A notable example is the song 'The Principal' by Melanie Martinez, in which she addresses her concerns about government and politics. She refers to those in political power as the "Principal" and critiques their failure to uphold a fair and just society for the people they govern.

Conversely, music can also harm listeners, especially regarding specific themes. "When people discuss how rap music with explicit themes can negatively impact the youth, that's the influence they're referencing. In this way, music significantly affects society, even unconsciously.

The emotions conveyed in the music we consume shape our thoughts," suggests Reyes. Like the positive aspects of music, there are also negative consequences, particularly for young, impressionable children. Listening to music can potentially exacerbate mental health issues, as previously mentioned, although an artist singing about similar emotions and situations can also serve as a source of hope. Yet, it can equally deepen feelings of distress.

It's crucial to be mindful when listening to songs during intense emotional states, and even more essential to recognize that dwelling on those negative emotions, despite their familiarity, is unhealthy. "Music featuring aggressive or harmful lyrics can influence listeners' behavior and perception, particularly among adolescents and young adults. Research indicates a correlation between exposure to music with violent or misogynistic themes and an increase in aggressive thoughts and behaviours," notes the website of Lifeline Rehab, a state-of-the-art facility for treating alcoholism, drug addiction, and psychiatric disorders located in Bani Gala, Islamabad. Although it has pros and cons, music is essential to society and influences how culture is shaped today. Ask anyone, and they can rant about how their favorite artists make them feel — that is the reality of music. Music can make or break society, and its significance will remain for years.

- Music has always reflected society, with cultural and historical contexts influencing the development of musical styles and genres. From blues to hip-hop, every genre has roots in the culture and identity of the people who created it. This blog will examine the role of culture and identity in music and how they shape the music we hear today. One key factor influencing music is what is popular in society. Music is a commercial enterprise, so it must cater to the tastes and interests of those who consume it. What is popular in society determines what type of music is created and promoted. For example, the rise of rock and roll in the 1950s was a response to the growing youth culture of the time, with young people looking for music that spoke to their experiences and emotions. Culture and identity also play a significant role in developing musical styles.

- Music is a way for people to express themselves and their cultural identities, whether through the rhythms and beats of African drumming or the twang of a country guitar. Different cultures have different musical traditions and ways of expressing themselves, which continue to shape the music we hear today. Historical events and movements also influence the development of music. For example, the civil rights movement in the 1960s profoundly impacted music, with artists like Nina Simone and Sam Cooke using their music to call attention to social injustice and promote equality. Similarly, the rise of punk rock in the 1970s was a response to the political and economic turmoil of the time, with bands like The Clash and The Sex Pistols using their music to express their frustration and anger at the establishment.

In addition to reflecting society, music also has the power to shape it. Music can catalyze social and political change, with artists using their platform to raise awareness about important issues and inspire people to act. For example, Bob Dylan's "Blowin' in the Wind" became an anthem for the civil rights movement, with its powerful lyrics calling for racial equality and an end to discrimination. Music reflects society, culture, and identity. It is influenced by what is popular in society, cultural traditions, historical events, and movements. By examining the role of culture and exploring identity in music, we can better understand how music shapes and reflects the world around us. As music listeners and creators, we can use music to inspire change and create a positive social impact. Music serves as a powerful mirror to societal moods and changes, often reflecting the dominant emotions, concerns, and cultural shifts of a specific period through its themes, lyrics, and style, as well as the emergence of new genres, essentially acting as a chronicle of history and social evolution.

Key Ways Music Reflects Societal Moods And Changes

Thematic Content: Lyrics often directly address social issues, political unrest, personal struggles, and societal values, giving insight into people's thoughts and feelings.

Genre Evolution: New music genres frequently respond to social changes, reflecting evolving societal attitudes and tastes. For example, the emergence of punk rock in the 1970s mirrored feelings of disillusionment and rebellion among youth.

Protest Music: Songs specifically created to address social injustices and advocate for change can become powerful tools for activism and mobilizing movements.

Cultural Influences: As societies become more interconnected, music incorporates elements from different cultures, creating hybrid genres that reflect the blending of diverse societal perspectives.

Historical Context

Examining music within its historical context can reveal how it reflects major events, societal upheavals, and shifts in power dynamics.

Examples of Music Reflecting Societal Moods:

The Great Depression Era: Blues music often expressed themes of hardship, poverty, and despair, reflecting the economic struggles of the time.

Civil Rights Movement: Soul and gospel music played a vital role in the movement, with songs like "We Shall Overcome" conveying hope and resilience.

Feminist Movement: Female artists started expressing themes of gender equality and empowerment through their music, contributing to the feminist discourse.

Post-9/11 Era: Music often reflected anxieties about terrorism and national security, incorporating themes of fear and uncertainty.

Theology: God blessed the nation of Israel with prophets and psalmists who wrote about God's greatness, faithfulness, wrath, love, grace, aseity, omniscience, omnipotence, and messianic prophecies. King David, the most prominent among them, wrote and sang songs about human frailty and dependency on God.

One of my favorite Psalms comes from the post-exilic period, where the writer expressed concern about the Babylonians asking for Zion's songs. He resisted singing Yahweh's music in strange lands, giving voice to how the Israelites perceived their master and reflecting that their music represented the nation of Israel.

Lyrics often directly address social issues, political unrest, personal struggles, and societal values, giving insight into people's thoughts and feelings.

About the Author

Emmanuel Victor Opasola popularly called *Apostle of Love* is a Nigerian clergy whose vision is to herald apostolic existence in the body of Christ at large. He believes that we are in the last days and the present day church must return to the ways of the early church. He seeks to see a rise of young men like himself who share the burden of the rebirth of the first apostolic cultures.

He has an apostolic community in Nigeria where communal lifestyle as in the early church is being practiced. He is a conservative and upholds the belief that Christians must live in moderation because the coming of the Lord is near.

CHAPTER 9

FAMILY DYNAMICS AND PERSONAL DEVELOPMENT

Bola and Folu were born a few hours apart, but their experiences growing up could not be any more contrasting. Bola's parents raised him in a caring and nurturing environment. He never saw his parents argue and was encouraged to share his thoughts during family discussions. He had modelled for him what it meant to be studious, disciplined, and productive. On the other hand, Folu had to endure a toxic upbringing. His parents fought openly, and he was often caught in their strife. He did not have a voice in the family and grew up with little confidence in his capabilities and worth.

The truth is, no one has the power to choose when and where they are born or the family environment in which they are raised. Yet, the experiences one has in the early years have a degree of impact on how one's life will eventually turn out. The dynamics within a family can make or mar a child's destiny, giving the child a great start to life or leaving him or her to play catch-up.

Family is often referred to as the bedrock of society. Within the family unit, individuals first experience relationships, develop their identity, and learn about the world. The dynamics of a family—the patterns of interaction and communication between its members—play a pivotal role in shaping a child's personal development.

When a child turns 18, their personal growth trajectory is often set on either the positive or negative side of the spectrum. I want to explore how family dynamics influence personal development and offer practical tips for overcoming challenges and fostering growth regardless of one's experience growing up.

The Impact of Toxic Family Environments

Negative family dynamics, such as emotional neglect, constant criticism, and toxic interactions, have a cumulative effect on personal development. Children raised in such environments often grapple with low self-esteem, unresolved emotional wounds, and a lack of direction. For instance, a child subjected to frequent criticism may internalise a belief that they are inherently flawed or incapable, leading to a fear of failure and hesitancy in pursuing opportunities.

Emotional neglect—the failure to provide adequate emotional support and validation—can leave a child feeling unseen and undervalued. This can be manifested in adulthood as difficulties in forming healthy relationships, managing emotions, or asserting oneself. Similarly, growing up in an atmosphere of constant conflict or unpredictability can result in heightened anxiety and a tendency to avoid challenges due to fear of adverse outcomes.

Over time, these effects can stifle a child's growth, leaving them ill-equipped to face the demands of adulthood. They may lack essential skills such as emotional regulation, problem-solving, and resilience, making navigating personal and professional landscapes harder.

The Power of Nurturing and Affirming Environments

In contrast, nurturing family environments foster positive personal development. Children raised in a love, respect, and affirmation climate develop a strong sense of self-worth and confidence. Parents who model healthy behaviours, such as effective communication, empathy, and perseverance, instill these traits in their children.

For example, a family that prioritises education and intellectual curiosity can inspire a child to value lifelong learning. Parents who encourage open dialogue and validate their children's emotions help them build emotional intelligence and self-awareness. Such environments also teach children to view mistakes as opportunities for growth rather than insurmountable failures.

In nurturing families, children are more likely to develop the skills, awareness, and motivation needed to independently continue their personal development journey. These early experiences lay a solid foundation for a fulfilling and successful life.

The Role of Family in Shaping Skills and Habits

Family dynamics affect a child's emotional and psychological well-being and influence the development of practical skills and habits. For instance, a child who observes their parents reading regularly or engaging in meaningful discussions may develop an appreciation for knowledge and self-improvement. Similarly, a household that emphasises accountability and self-discipline will encourage a child to take responsibility for their actions and strive for excellence.

Conversely, children from toxic environments may struggle with motivation or lack essential life skills. For example, a child who grows up in a chaotic or neglectful household may not learn the importance of time management, goal setting, or self-care. These deficits can hinder their ability to succeed in various aspects of life.

Taking Responsibility for Personal Growth

There is more to Bola and Folu's story. During their Sixth Form years, Bola associated with friends who enticed him into a lifestyle of drugs. Before long, his academic performance plunged, and he broke his parents' heart when he dropped out of school. Folu finished high school in flying colours. He had ambitious friends who inspired him to develop a habit of reading and self-improvement. When he was admitted to the university to study law, his proud parents drove him to his campus on resumption day.

What a paradox! While family dynamics undeniably shape personal development, they do not define one's destiny. Every individual has the opportunity and responsibility to take the reins of their life and chart their path. Though understandable, blaming the past or one's upbringing is ultimately unproductive. Instead, the past should be used as fuel for growth and transformation.

It is empowering to acknowledge that personal development is a lifelong journey regardless of one's starting point. Taking ownership of this journey requires a willingness to learn, adapt, and persevere. By focusing on what can be controlled and working to overcome limitations, individuals can rise above their circumstances and create a fulfilling life.

Practical Tips for Personal Development

Whether you come from a nurturing or challenging background, you can choose a winning path and an admirable future. The following actionable tips are universal strategies that will help you foster personal and professional growth irrespective of your background or upbringing:

1. Read Widely: Books offer a wealth of knowledge and perspectives. Reading regularly can expand your understanding of the world, inspire creativity, and improve critical thinking skills.

2. Seek Mentors: Surround yourself with people who inspire and challenge you to grow. A mentor can provide guidance, encouragement, and valuable insights based on their experiences.

3. Practice Self-Reflection: Evaluate your thoughts, actions, and progress. Journaling or meditating can help you gain clarity and identify areas for improvement.

4. Set Goals: Establish clear, achievable objectives for your personal and professional life. Break these goals into smaller, actionable steps to maintain focus and track progress.

5. Develop Emotional Intelligence: Work on understanding and managing your emotions and empathizing with others. This skill is crucial for building healthy relationships and navigating challenges.

6. Invest in Continuous Learning: Pursue opportunities to acquire new skills or knowledge, whether through formal education, online courses, or hands-on experiences.

7. Surround Yourself with Positivity: Cultivate relationships with people who uplift and motivate you. Limit interactions with those who drain your energy or perpetuate negativity.

8. Focus on Health and Well-Being: A healthy body supports a healthy mind. To enhance well-being, prioritise physical activity, balanced nutrition, and sufficient sleep.

   Family dynamics undeniably play a crucial role in shaping personal development, influencing everything from self-esteem to life skills. However, no matter the circumstances of one's upbringing, personal growth is within everyone's reach. By taking responsibility for them

By developing and adopting practical strategies, we can all overcome the limitations of a horrid past and unlock our full potential, just like Folu did.

About the Author

Tokunbo Emmanuel is a visionary publisher, a scribal prophet, a writing coach, a platform builder, and the CEO of *Sophos Books Ltd.* With over 35 years' experience as a publisher, Tokunbo is a valuable resource within the African scribal community.

He is passionate about contributing to development in the African continent through the power of the written word. Tokunbo is the author of many transformative books, including *'The Shift of a Lifetime'* and *'God is Mindful of You'*.

He is happily married to Linda, and they are blessed with three children, Destiny, Daniel, and David.

CHAPTER 10

MONEY, MONEY, MONEY

A Short Reflection

"So, what's all this about money, son?"

"What?"

"I heard you withering on, worrying in your head. (As if worrying ever changed anything!)"

"OK, Father. I have these bills and expenses, and I can't see how I will pay them."

"Food, clothes, housing costs - that sort of thing?"
"Spot on, Father, and lots more. I don't know the specifics, but they seem to keep coming daily."

"Right. And you thought I'd leave you alone to sort those, did you, because I've got lots of ***Very Important Things*** on my plate just now, like saving the world, shaping governments, stuff like that?"

"I suppose I sort of did, though I hadn't put it into words."

"Remind me, son, how much did My Son Jesus seem to worry about money?"

"Um. Now you ask, I can't think of even one mention of Him doing so. How did He manage that, Father, especially during His amazing 3-year public adventure when He wasn't earning a living?"

"Do you remember what I prompted Matthew to write about being concerned about food, clothes, housing costs, etc., in what you call Chapter 6?"

"Oh yes! I know this one, Father. We love to quote it. All about seeking first Your Kingdom and Righteousness and all those other practical things will be taken care of, because you know what we need."

"Yes, son... And what do you suppose that means, about My Kingdom and Righteousness?"

"I always thought that meant being busy with church, giving money to that, and missions, trying to get other people to believe in Jesus. Being a bit of a religious nut, I suppose, if I'm honest."

"So many of you think that way and, bless you, completely miss the point, again... Oh, the joys of being a parent! As so often, you think I'm looking for people who are good at ***Tick-Box*** religion, keeping up with external religious stuff. As if..."

"Huh?"

"Listen carefully, son. My Kingdom is in my children's hearts, as close as the air you breathe. It's about your heart's attitude and who's on your throne. If you allow me to lead you, in the driving seat through all your ordinary everyday living, with us doing life together, I'll ensure you have what you need when you need it. All the necessities of life will fall into place. To quote a TV ad, "Simples". And my promises to you are not nice and fluffy, they're solid granite in their certainty. Trusting Me, walking with Me, being wonderfully child-like free alongside Me, that's the nub of it."

"OK, Father, I think the light is beginning to dawn in this thick skull of mine. But how does that work out with my money? What does it look like?"

"Your money? Nah, it's all Mine if I'm really in the driving seat of your life. When I nudge you to give away, to save, to spend on some flowers for someone who needs cheering up, to invest, or maybe to *roll up** some money and stick it in a wire fence at an airport, you do it. You'll find that My economics doesn't work on paper, but, oh Boy, do they work when you try them! I am so very good at making things add up right. And you'll find it's fun, this adventuring with me. (As well as some nail-biting adventures to train you to trust me more and enjoy more and more freedom!)"

"Wow, that's brilliant, Father! Anything else you want to say to me about all this?"

"Just one. If you let me use your money, I'll let you use Mine!

(*Some friends of mine found this out on their return from their honeymoon abroad, with no money for breakfast!)

If you allow Me to
lead you, in the driving
seat through all your
ordinary everyday
living, with us doing
life together, I'll ensure
you have what you
need when you need it.

About the Author

Tim Simpson's story is a powerful testament to God's sovereignty and love. In 1966, at just 15 years old, Tim's life was dramatically changed when God convicted him of sin and revealed His love in a profound way. Without any prior Christian background, Tim was suddenly and irreversibly drawn into God's Kingdom.

His encounter was marked by intense conviction, desperate prayer, and an overwhelming sense of forgiveness. From that moment on, Tim's life was forever changed, and he began a journey of deepening his relationship with God. His story highlights the transformative power of God's grace and the importance of personal faith.

PART TWO

IMPACT

Chapter 11

A RECONCILIATION OR REUNION WITH A LOVED ONE

"The Walk Back."

It started with a voicemail.

"Hey… It's Mom. Just calling to see if you'll be around for your dad's birthday. It'd mean a lot to him. To us. Hope you're doing okay."

She hung up before the beep even finished. No rambling. No guilt trip. Just that quiet little olive branch, extended with shaky fingers. I listened to it three times before deleting it. Then I packed a bag.

It had been almost three years since I'd been home. Not just physically, but home. The kind where you sit at the table and pour coffee without asking, where you know where the aspirin is, where your last name echoes off the walls in old stories and inside jokes. We stopped talking after the fight with Dad—well, a series of fights. Some loud, some silent, all of them exhausting.

I blamed him for not showing up when I needed him most, and he blamed me for walking away like it was easy.

But grief is never simple, and when we lost my sister, none of us knew what to do with ourselves. So we all retreated into separate rooms. Doors shut. Conversations unfinished. And now here I was, on a highway back to a house that hadn't changed much, even if we had.

The front door stuck, and I had to put my shoulder into it before it gave way. Same creaky hinge, same faint smell of coffee grounds and old wood. The dog—a new dog now—barked once, then stared at me like it knew my name. Mom came out of the kitchen with her hands still wet. She looked like she'd aged five years instead of three. Less colour in her hair, more caution in her smile.

"Hey," she said.

"Hey."

She hugged me as if I were a memory she wasn't sure would remain intact. I allowed myself to sink into it. I didn't realize how much I needed that until I felt her hand on the back of my neck, just like she used to when I was a child with a fever.

"He's out in the shed," she said as we pulled apart. "Fixing the radio again. Go easy, okay?"

I nodded. She didn't need to say more. The shed was his sanctuary, where he went to escape the noise- the same noise I brought into the house the night I packed up and left without looking back.

I stood at the edge of the back porch for a while before venturing out there. I watched him through the dusty window, hunched over his workbench as if he were trying to fix more than just wires.

The door creaked when I opened it, but he didn't turn around. "You still fighting with that old thing?" I asked.

He glanced over his shoulder, surprised, but not in the expected way. It felt as if he'd been waiting, hoping, and now that I was there, he didn't quite know how to respond. "Stubborn little bastard won't hold a signal," he said, fiddling with the dial. "Kind of like someone else I know." I smiled, just barely. He noticed.

"Figured you'd be out in the garage," he said, finally facing me.

"Garage got cleaned out. All my stuff's probably gone, huh?" He shrugged. "Some of it's still in boxes. I couldn't bring myself to toss it."

That hung between us, awkward and filled with unspoken thoughts. Then he gestured to a stool.

"Want to sit?"

I did.

The first twenty minutes passed with small talk: the weather, work, the damn radio. Then silence returned, the kind that stretches and dares you to break it.

"I didn't think you'd come," he said eventually, his eyes fixed on the floor.

"I almost didn't."

"Yeah. That makes sense."

More silence.

"I kept waiting for you to call," I said. "After everything... I thought you might try."

"I wanted to, " he paused. Every single day. But I figured you didn't want to hear from me."

"I didn't. Not at first. But time passes. Anger cools. Hurt doesn't, though; that just gets buried."

He nodded slowly, as if the weight of those words was something he understood too well.

"When she died," he started, then stopped. "When we lost her... I didn't know how to be anything other than angry. Angry at the world. At God. At myself. And you—"

"You were angry at me."

"I didn't know how else to deal with losing her. Then you left, and it felt like I lost both of you."

"I left because I couldn't breathe in that house anymore. Everything was hers. Her pictures, her shoes still by the door, her damn toothbrush. And you wouldn't talk. You just sat there silently, like it was a punishment for the rest of us."

His jaw tightened. "It was a punishment. But for me." The room stilled once again.

"I wanted to scream," I said. "I wanted to punch something. But whenever I tried to talk about her, you'd shut down. Like pretending she wasn't gone would bring her back."

"I couldn't say her name without falling apart. And I thought, who would hold it together if I fell apart?"

"You didn't hold anything together, Dad. We all just drifted." And there it was. Raw. Honest. Ugly.

But it didn't blow up this time. No shouting. No storming out. Just… sitting with it.

He looked over at me, eyes glassy.

"You think I don't miss her every day? That I don't hear her laugh in my sleep? That I don't still set the table for four by mistake?"

"I never said you didn't miss her. I just needed you to let me miss her with you. Not alone."

He blinked hard, then rubbed his hand over his face. "I didn't know how. I still don't."

"I know," I said. "Me neither. But maybe we could learn." After that, we sat there for a while, not talking, just existing. Two men, both missing the same person in different ways—a father and a son trying to find a way back to each other, not through apology but through honesty.

Dinner that night was simple—spaghetti and salad. Mom lit a candle in the middle of the table as if it were some offering to the moment. Dad and I talked more—not about everything, but enough to believe that the door we thought was shut forever might open again.

Later, after the dishes were done and Mom had gone to bed, Dad poured two whiskies and passed one to me. We sat on the porch, quiet again, but this time it felt peaceful. "You think she'd be mad at us?" he asked.

"No," I said. "She'd just be glad we're not being idiots anymore."

He chuckled. "Yeah. She always hated when we fought." "We fought a lot."

"We're a lot alike," he said, raising his glass slightly. "Stubborn bastards."

We clinked glasses and took a sip.

I slept in my old room that night. The posters were gone, and the bed creaked a little more than I remembered, but it felt like home in a way I hadn't felt in years. I lay there thinking about all the lost time and conversations we hadn't had. But I also thought about the ones we could still share. Dad was flipping pancakes at the stove when I came downstairs the following day.

"Happy birthday," I said.

He smiled. "Best gift I could've asked for."

Reconciliation isn't some grand moment. It's not tearful monologues or dramatic music swelling in the background. It's a series of small choices: a voicemail, a drive, a shared silence. The courage to say, I was hurt, and to hear, I hurt you too.

It's not about forgetting what broke. It's about deciding it's worth trying to fix.

And sometimes, it starts with just showing up.

About the Author

Olutunu Babalola-Daniel encountered God as a committed Christian 37 years ago. She is an intercessor, a teacher of the word, and a worshiper.

Over the years, Olutunu has assisted and pioneered church planting projects and worked as a bible-study teacher, youth leader, church administrator, treasurer, and trustee. Olutunu is passionate about pulling down strongholds and seeing captives set free from Satan's Kingdom through intense prayers. *'The Arsenal of the Christian'* is Olutunu's first writing project. In this book, she has used her life experiences to explore all the weapons the Lord has equipped every believer with for living a spirit-filled and purposeful life.

Olutunu currently attends *RCCG Impact Centre Church* in Bicester. She is married to Rotimi Patrick Daniel.

CHAPTER 12

THE FIRST TIME YOU MAKE A BIG, LIFE-ALTERING DECISION

The first time I made a significant, life-altering decision for myself was when I met my husband, David. Looking back, it was a moment that changed the course of my life and defined the person I would become. It was a decision rooted in courage, faith, and love—and it remains one of the most transformative choices I've ever made.

To truly appreciate the magnitude of this decision, it is crucial to understand where I was in my life when David walked in. At that time, I was in my late twenties, navigating the uncertainties of adulthood. I held a stable job as a nurse, had good friends, and enjoyed a supportive family, but something inside me felt incomplete. I had spent years following others' expectations, doing what I believed was "right" or "acceptable," but I had never truly stepped out and decided purely for myself.

Enter David. We met at a mutual friend's gathering, and from the moment he introduced himself, there was something undeniably magnetic about him. David possessed a rare blend of confidence and humility. He carried himself efficiently, instantly making everyone around him feel comfortable. His smile was warm, his laughter infectious, and his ability to connect with people was something I had never encountered before. David, a chemist, property developer, and investor, exuded a depth of ambition and drive that intrigued me. I was drawn to him, yet I also felt apprehensive. Was I ready to open my heart to someone? Could I trust myself to make such a significant decision?

Our first conversation was simple yet profound. We talked about everything—from our favourite books and music to our dreams and fears. David listened intently, not just to respond but to truly understand me. At that moment, I realized I had never felt so seen, valued, and understood.

It was as if he had reached into the depths of my soul and touched something that had been dormant for years. I didn't know it then, but this was the beginning of a journey that would lead me to make one of the most significant decisions of my life.

We fell in love at first sight, and everything moved quickly yet naturally. Six weeks after the meeting, David proposed. His confidence in us gave me the courage to trust my feelings. Ten months later, we were married in a beautiful ceremony surrounded by family and friends. It was a whirlwind, but it felt right. It felt like destiny.

As our relationship developed, I found myself at a crossroads. Up until that point, I had always prioritised safety and predictability. I had built walls around my heart, convincing myself that vulnerability was a weakness. But David challenged that notion. He showed me that vulnerability was a strength and a necessary ingredient for growth and connection. He encouraged me to step outside my comfort zone, embrace the unknown, and take risks.

One of the defining moments in our early relationship came about six months after we started dating. David had a light-bulb moment and wanted us to marry immediately. He did not see the point in prolonging our courtship as families had met. Our mentors approved our relationship, and everything worked in our favour. However, I became somewhat apprehensive. The idea terrified me. Leaving my familiar surroundings, friends, family—everything I had known—to start a new life with someone I hardly knew, but it was a leap of faith unlike anything I had ever taken. Saying yes to David meant saying yes to love, growth, and the unknown. It meant trusting myself and trusting him. It wasn't an easy decision. I spent countless nights wrestling with my fears and doubts. What if it didn't work out? What if I was making a mistake? But each time those questions arose; I reminded myself of who David was and how he made me feel. He was my safe place, my partner, and my greatest cheerleader. With him, I felt empowered to take on the world.

The moment I told David I would move with him remains one of the most significant moments of my life. His face lit up with relief and joy, and he pulled me into the kind of embrace that makes you feel like you're exactly where you're meant to be. From that moment on, we began planning our new life together. It wasn't just about the logistics of living together but about building a foundation for our future. Deep down, I knew that this was my moment. This was the time to decide for myself, choose the life I wanted, and embrace the possibilities ahead.

To reassure me, David began by putting his thinking hat on and writing a plan to make us achieve this goal in record time. He knew I was visual and that writing a solid plan on paper would be a faith-booster. As such, we sat down together at the dining table and planned how to achieve the goal of getting married within a short time. We reached a compromise of 10 months and saved half our monthly wages to accomplish this goal. We convinced our families that it could be done and went about planning. We got divine help and favour along the way, and everything seemed to fall into place instantly.

I remember that the first place I walked into for my wedding dress and the first few gowns I tried on fitted me instantly. It felt like the wedding gown and accessories, including the shoes, were already waiting for me. In addition, we received very generous support from the leadership and church members. Several volunteers gladly offered to sponsor various aspects of the wedding. Alas! 10 months went by so quickly, and before we knew it, we walked down the aisle, beaming with joy and faith. It was the best day of our lives.

Moving in with David was both exhilarating and challenging. We faced our share of struggles—adjusting to a new environment, finding jobs, and building a community from scratch. But through it all, we had each other. David's unwavering support and love gave me the strength to navigate the uncertainties. He believed in me even when I doubted myself, and that belief became the cornerstone of our relationship.

As time passed, I began to see how this decision had transformed me. I was no longer the person who played it safe or avoided risks. I had become someone who embraced change, who saw challenges as opportunities for growth, and who valued love and connection above all else. God had used David to change my life and helped me discover who I was.

Twenty-eight years later, our life together is a testament to the power of love, faith, and perseverance. We have three wonderful, grown-up children who bring us immense joy and pride. As christians, our faith has been the cornerstone of our marriage, helping us navigate countless challenges and celebrate many victories. There have been moments of struggle and many times of wanting to give up on the relationship from both sides, but our commitment to each other and to God has always seen us through.

Our relationship continued to grow, and we overcame many adversities together. Standing there with him, saying "yes" to a lifetime together, felt like the natural culmination of the journey we had started when I made that first life-altering decision. Our wedding celebrated love, resilience, and the power of choosing each other daily.

Today, as I reflect on that pivotal moment, I am grateful. Meeting David and deciding to build a life with him was not just about finding a partner; it was about finding myself. It was about realizing that the most significant decisions we make are the ones that come from the heart. It was about learning to trust myself and embrace the beauty of the unknown.

David and I have built a life rich with love, laughter, and purpose. We have faced challenges, celebrated victories, and grown together in ways I could never have imagined. Through it all, I am reminded of the power of that first decision—to take a chance on love, step out in faith, and choose a life that is true to who I am.

Meeting David and choosing to be with him was the first time I made a big, life-altering decision for myself. It required courage, faith, and vulnerability. It changed my life forever; I would make it again in a heartbeat.

About the Author

Lydia Olorunniwo is a passionate servant of God and founder of *Kingdom Love International Network (KLINE)*, a ministry focused on encouraging and sharpening believers' faith worldwide. Her mission is to help people live in the supernatural and fulfill their divine purposes. *KLINE* offers virtual prayer meetings, intercession hubs, and support for those in need. Lydia mentors youths and women, equipping them to discover their purpose and walk in their divine assignment. With her husband, Pastor David, she builds a home centered on prayer, purpose, and hospitality. Her message emphasizes being complete in Christ and discovering one's identity and gifts.

CHAPTER 13

IMMERSING YOURSELF IN A NEW CULTURE OR WAY OF LIFE

Introduction

Immersing oneself in a new culture is a transformative experience that broadens horizons, deepens understanding, and fosters personal growth. It involves navigating cultural differences, overcoming language barriers, and adjusting to new social norms, requiring openness, humility, and resilience.

A. The Initial Encounter: Culture Shock and Adaptation

Experiencing a new culture can be overwhelming and lead to culture shock, a natural response to unfamiliar environments where familiar cultural cues and social norms no longer apply.

The Stages of Culture Shock

Culture shock typically unfolds in several stages, each with experiences and challenges.

Honeymoon Stage: First, the new culture may excite and fascinate you. Everything seems fresh, and the differences between your culture and the new one are captivating and thrilling. This stage is marked by curiosity and a desire to explore and learn.

Negotiation Stage: As the initial excitement fades, the reality of cultural differences begins to set in. You might start to feel frustrated or alienated by the challenges of navigating a different language, social norms, and daily routines. Misunderstandings can occur, leading to feelings of homesickness or discomfort.

Adjustment Stage: Over time, you adapt to the new culture. You learn to navigate the differences and better understand the cultural context. You may establish routines and build relationships, making the new environment more familiar and manageable.

Adaptation Stage: Eventually, you reach a stage of adaptation where you feel more comfortable and integrated into the new culture. While challenges may still arise, you have developed the skills and confidence to handle them. You can fully appreciate the new culture's nuances and complexities at this point, and it begins to feel like a second home.

B. Overcoming Culture Shock

Overcoming culture shock requires practical strategies and mindset shifts. Learning the language and understanding local customs are essential. Maintaining an open mind and humility helps you embrace differences and appreciate the richness of human cultures.

Language: The Gateway to Understanding

Language is one of the most significant barriers when immersing yourself in a new culture, but it also serves as a gateway to deeper understanding and connection. Learning the local language, even at a conversational level, can significantly enhance your experience by allowing you to communicate more effectively, grasp cultural nuances, and forge relationships with locals.

C. **The Importance of Language in Cultural Immersion**

"Language is deeply connected to culture, reflecting the values and beliefs of a community. Learning a new language provides insight into how people think, communicate, and relate to one another. It also opens doors to more authentic experiences and deeper connections, fostering meaningful friendships and a richer understanding of the culture."

D. **Strategies for Language Learning**

Learning a new language can be challenging, but several strategies can make the process more manageable and enjoyable.

Immersive Learning: Surround yourself with the language as much as possible. Listen to local radio stations, watch TV shows or movies, read books or newspapers, and converse with native speakers. The more you expose yourself to the language, the quicker you pick it up.

Language Exchange: Participate in language exchange programs where you can practice speaking the language with native speakers while helping them learn your language. This enhances your language skills and offers an opportunity for cultural exchange and building friendships.

Language Classes: Enroll in language classes to build a strong foundation in grammar, vocabulary, and pronunciation. Formal instruction can enhance your learning and give you the confidence to practice the language in real-life situations.

Practice Daily: Consistency is vital when learning a new language. Practice speaking, listening, reading, and writing every day. Each culture has its social norms and etiquette. Understanding and respecting these norms is crucial for successful cultural immersion.

E. Greetings and Communication

Greetings vary across cultures, from handshakes to bows, hugs, or kisses. Understanding appropriate greetings and cultural norms around eye contact and communication styles is crucial for positive interactions and avoiding miscommunication.

Dining Etiquette

Awareness of the varying dining customs and etiquette across cultures is essential. For example, in China, leaving a small amount of food on your plate shows that you are full and have been provided with enough food, while in many Western cultures, finishing your plate is a sign of appreciation. Understanding local dining etiquette helps you feel more comfortable in social situations, shows respect for the culture, and provides insight into the culture's values and traditions.

Gift-Giving

Gift-giving customs vary across cultures, with specific rules about types of gifts, presentation, and reception. For example, in Japan, presenting gifts with both hands is customary as a sign of respect. Understanding these customs can help navigate social interactions and learn about cultural values.

Building Relationships and Community

One of the most rewarding aspects of immersing yourself in a new culture is the opportunity to build relationships and become part of a new community.

These relationships provide a deeper understanding of the culture and can lead to lifelong friendships. However, building relationships in a new culture requires effort, patience, and cultural sensitivity.

Finding Common Ground

Establishing common ground is crucial for connecting in a new culture. This can involve finding shared interests like hobbies, sports, or cultural activities or having everyday conversations about food, weather, or family. Engaging in local events, festivals, or community activities is another way to build relationships and immerse yourself in the culture. These activities can help you feel like you belong and strengthen your connection to the culture.

Overcoming Challenges in Building Relationships

Building relationships in a new culture can be challenging due to cultural and language barriers. It's essential to be patient and adaptable to different communication styles. Understanding cultural expectations around friendships and social interactions is also key to managing expectations and approaching relationships with an open mind.

The Rewards of Building Cross-Cultural Relationships

Building cross-cultural relationships during cultural immersion is rewarding despite its challenges. These relationships provide valuable insights into a culture's values, beliefs, and way of life and offer opportunities for cultural exchange. Moreover, they can lead to personal growth by exposing individuals to new perspectives, challenging assumptions and biases, and fostering greater cross-cultural understanding and respect.

Personal Growth and Reflection

Immersing yourself in a new culture is not just about learning new customs and languages; it's also a journey of personal growth and self-reflection. As you navigate the challenges of cultural immersion, you are likely to learn as much about yourself as you do about the new culture.

Expanding Your Worldview

One of the most significant aspects of personal growth during cultural immersion is the expansion of your worldview. By immersing yourself in a different culture, you gain a deeper understanding of the diversity of human experiences and the various ways people live, think, and relate to the world. This broader perspective can foster greater open-mindedness, tolerance, and appreciation for the richness of human cultures.

For example, living in a culture that prioritises community and family over individual achievement may challenge your assumptions about success. And happiness. You may appreciate the value of close-knit communities and the importance of social bonds, leading to a shift in your values and priorities.

- **Developing Resilience and Adaptability**
  Cultural immersion fosters resilience and adaptability. Adjusting to a new culture requires developing coping strategies and problem-solving skills. Overcoming language barriers and adapting to social norms builds the confidence needed to handle unfamiliar situations, translating into greater self-assurance for new challenges in life.

- **Reflecting on Your Own Identity**
  Immersing yourself in a new culture often prompts reflection on your cultural identity and values. As you engage with a different way of life, you may question

or re-evaluate your beliefs, assumptions, and cultural practices. This process of self-reflection can lead to a deeper understanding of your identity and a more nuanced view of your cultural background.

For example, you might gain a new appreciation for aspects of your own culture that you previously took for granted, or you might identify areas where your beliefs or behaviours have been influenced by cultural norms that you now see in a different light. This self-awareness is essential to personal growth and can lead to a more authentic and reflective approach to life.

Conclusion

Immersing yourself in a new culture or way of life is a transformative experience that offers countless opportunities for learning, growth, and connection. While the process can be challenging, involving culture shock, language barriers, and the need to navigate unfamiliar social norms, it also provides a unique chance to expand your worldview, develop resilience, and gain a deeper understanding of yourself and others.

By approaching cultural immersion with an open mind, a willingness to learn, and a respect for the diversity of human experience, you can make the most of this journey and emerge with a richer, more nuanced perspective on the world. Whether through travel, study, or community engagement, the experience of living in a new culture can leave a lasting impact on your life, shaping the way you see the world and your place within it.

About the Author

Olutunu Babalola-Daniel encountered God as a committed Christian 37 years ago. She is an intercessor, a teacher of the word, and a worshiper.

Over the years, Olutunu has assisted and pioneered church planting projects and worked as a bible-study teacher, youth leader, church administrator, treasurer, and trustee. Olutunu is passionate about pulling down strongholds and seeing captives set free from Satan's Kingdom through intense prayers. *'The Arsenal of the Christian'* is Olutunu's first writing project. In this book, she has used her life experiences to explore all the weapons the Lord has equipped every believer with for living a spirit-filled and purposeful life.

Olutunu currently attends *RCCG Impact Centre Church* in Bicester. She is married to Rotimi Patrick Daniel.

CHAPTER 14

THE DEATH OF A LOVED ONE

I see her almost every day in my sleep; it's been three weeks, but I have yet to recover from the shock. It still looks like a dream; I wish it were a lie. Today, it was her in my dreams that woke me up again; yesterday, it was her hug that woke me up. I realised she holds a space in my heart that now I don't know who can fill it up. I have yet to wrap up my mind about the fact that she is no longer with us. I watched them put her down into Mother Earth with my eyes swollen, but her spirit is with me everywhere I go. We were not married; she was only my cousin, but I loved her like my daughter. The memories keep playing in my mind; no doubt, it is why I keep seeing her in my sleep, but I believe it is more than mere thoughts of her that have clogged my mind because what I saw this morning is not what my mind could have made up.

I woke up with my head swollen and my eyes reddish. I saw myself at a big conference, and we retired into our rooms. I decided to check on my folks in the other room. While I was there monitoring them all, with different conversations ongoing like in a market because there were quite a handful of teenagers and youths, and like in real-time, I was going with the flow as I am a sanguine personality, I was cracking jokes with them when all of a sudden, we heard screams because someone had alerted a few of them of a sparkling little light and questionings were ongoing about who lit this light, as I also turned to check because this had caught everyone's attention. As I looked, I saw a little candle.

Still, suddenly, it was her standing there, and it seemed she had revealed herself to me, whereas no one else was seeing her except this small light that they did not understand. Immediately, I saw her; she was standing by the window just opposite the doorway where I had stood; the candle I saw was on the window. I moved to hold her hands again as I usually do, but then a hand pulled me back, and it seemed as though someone else had seen her in the room other than me, but I was struggling and screaming, per adventure these unknown hands would leave me to hold her again. I was working with this unknown hand, and I could hear myself screaming, *"She is my baby girl. She could not hurt me, leave me with her!"* but these unknown hands wouldn't let me go and... Pop! I woke up and realised it was only a dream, yet I wished she were confirmed again.

It feels like yesterday; it still hurts to have lost her to the cold arms of death; she was a young, vibrant lady who had just finished her youth service last year in Sokoto, Nigeria. Her sojourn in Sokoto marked a turning point where everything about her changed. What led to her early grave affected her. Her education had been a struggle; she began in the village before she returned to the city, where she continued and eventually gained admission into the university to study accounting upon graduation.

The Nigerian Youth Service Scheme posted her to Sokoto State. We had lots of struggles accepting that she should go to serve in that faraway land, which is the northern side of the country, and we stayed in the southern part.

She insisted she would love to take the adventure because she is such an adventurous lady, the vibe in the house is jovial, and she unites the family with her jokes, just like me. She took so much after me, and you will always see her wrapped herself around me every time she gets the opportunity; interestingly, her mother has four girls, and she is the second, and for this reason, the girls see me as their big brother, and they always want me to come around. This has made us so fond of each other, and I am seen as the brother they never had. We would walk the street at night, crack bedtime jokes, and lie together; I would watch them sleep, then step out to my room; oftentimes, they would sleep in my room in their house with me.

She decided to travel far north and called me to pray with her and give my blessings. I also love adventure; I feel she took this virtue from me. She always loved to act like the man in the house. She was the strongest among them. Fast forward, she landed at Sokoto, and she got a very decent posting to a hotel; while being there, this terrible illness that eventually took her life ten months later popped up. She did not fall ill anyhow before this time; towards the end of her service year, she discovered breathing was getting difficult sometimes; when she complained to her mother through a video call because the mother is a nurse, she was pretty confused if it could be asthma because she never had it before now. We pushed her to return home after the service year, although she told us about the hotel management retaining her to work.

She returned to the southwest in April of the following year after completing her youth service in December; we believe the dust in the north and the heat that made her stay in the air conditioning rooms triggered asthma. Every day, the mother bites her tongue and fingers, wishing she had not allowed her to travel to the north. Everyone is in disbelief, and we hoped she had not gone to an area where this unimaginable, terrible illness could have been triggered within her. We know firsthand how terrible asthma can be because our grandpa died of asthma, but he lived for over a hundred years. We couldn't calculate his exact age because he was the oldest man in the village by the time he died about twenty-two years ago. We know that if not for this asthma, he could have lived longer. We know the pain firsthand, but we never knew her mother could have been a carrier and passed it to this girl; up until this asthma was triggered in her, we all thought we had overcome the ordeal of asthma in the family.

She battled with it extensively after she came back from youth service again for about five months until she gave up the ghost. I was dumbfounded when I received the call that evening that she was between life and death. She was rushed to the hospital as her condition changed drastically that evening. Her mother took her to her clinic that morning and watched her enjoy herself. It was a day filled with laughter as she chatted excitedly, playing all around, when suddenly she complained of a slight inability to breathe again. She took her to the bed, connected her to the drip, gave her injections, and she was responding well again. That evening, the mother called the father to pick them up and take them home in his car.

Just as the father arrived and they took her up from the bed, her condition changed immediately; this was strange because she was already well, and the mother was confused. They rushed her to a bigger hospital immediately, and the doctor rushed in to attend to her; the way her father drove to the hospital that evening was crazy. The doctor was trying to get her to use the oxygen for breathing when I received the call that has broken me down till now. The doctor and the nurses tried their best for about an hour until they lost her; by the time I got to the hospital, she was gone. I hugged one of our fathers, crying on his shoulder, and I rushed in to look at her cadaver. I saw her lifeless. I began screaming and shouting, and everyone was holding me down. I wounded myself that evening. It was already late, and there was nowhere to take her for burial; we couldn't embalm her either because we had informed the hospital that we would be burying her immediately. We were confused about what to do. It was a painful death, and we had to carry the parents' home because, according to tradition, they shouldn't look again at her dead body, and they also couldn't follow us to bury her the next day.

We couldn't get to the place where we buried her that evening again because everyone we called to use their burial ground and the diggers couldn't be reached on time; we decided to take her to church and keep her until morning; this made me happy because I felt I would pray, and she would return. I prayed all night, hoping for her to sneeze again and wake up, when suddenly, in the middle of the night, I heard her voice telling me, " My elder brother, I have become like the wind. I wept and wept when I listened to this; I cried, I said no, and I kept begging God all night, refusing to back down, but she never returned; we took her early morning to a graveyard nearby to lay her remains there forever, and I cried and cried hoping something could still happen.

I woke up again this morning, three weeks later, and with my head swollen again, I began to sob all over. I was soaked in tears, and then I heard my door creak, and I thought a ghost had entered. I wanted to freak out, but I smiled, and I wished she were the one who had walked in again, but no one was there. I cried increasingly and began pondering my dream, trying to find meaning. Suddenly, I realised it was saying I had to let go of her so she could rest and that I should focus on my life and do great things in her memory. If she looked down from heaven, she would smile and be glad that her memory was righteous and blessed. I hope to have a girls' foundation in her name shortly.

Everyone is in
disbelief, and we hoped
she had not gone to
an area where this
unimaginable, terrible
illness could have been
triggered within her.

About the Author

Emmanuel Victor Opasola popularly called *Apostle of Love* is a Nigerian clergy whose vision is to herald apostolic existence in the body of Christ at large. He believes that we are in the last days and the present day church must return to the ways of the early church. He seeks to see a rise of young men like himself who share the burden of the rebirth of the first apostolic cultures.

He has an apostolic community in Nigeria where communal lifestyle as in the early church is being practiced. He is a conservative and upholds the belief that Christians must live in moderation because the coming of the Lord is near.

CHAPTER 15

BROADENED PERSPECTIVES

Adapting to a new culture or way of life can be both enriching and challenging, especially for families with children. As a Child and Family Therapist and a Youth Minister I often encourage families to view cultural transition as an opportunity for growth, resilience, and deeper connection. Whether relocating to a new country or embracing new values due to life changes, such as marriage, work, adoption, or faith shifts, children and parents alike benefit from intentional immersion.

Observation of the traditions, and unspoken social norms of your new environment, can be a starting point. This creates a sense of belonging and builds confidence, particularly in children who may struggle with feeling "different." Parents should model curiosity rather than fear, as it's also good to observe and learn.

In my field working closely with Christian families, I have witnessed the emotional and spiritual challenges that can arise when individuals or families are immersed in a new culture or way of life, whether due to migration, cross-cultural marriages, missions, adoption, or even a significant life transition stages within the same society, for example–a toddler becoming an Adolescent. While these changes often bring growth, they also call for deep intentionality and spiritual mentoring of this adult to be. From a biblical perspective, the concept of immersion in a new culture is not foreign.

Abraham was called out of his homeland to an unfamiliar land (Genesis 12), and Daniel had to live faithfully in Babylon without compromising his convictions. Jesus himself entered our world and culture as Emmanuel; "God with us" fully identifying with humanity while maintaining His divine nature.

Immersing yourself in a new culture can be both enriching and disorienting. For children, especially, the shift can impact their identity development, sense of belonging, and even their faith journey. Adults may find themselves questioning values, struggling to maintain traditions, or navigating internal conflicts between cultural expectations and spiritual convictions. In such transitions, family systems are also tested. Communication patterns, roles, rules and routines often change, which may trigger anxiety or confusion, particularly for young people.

I recall working with a Black family who had recently moved into the UK, one of the children facing peer pressure wanted to dress up in what her family and her faith calls indecent dressing, it almost cost the family's relationship until Mum realised it would be helpful if she express her concerns in a way that invites conversation rather than conflict. Over time, the child began to open up not just about her emotions but the peer pressure of wanting to belong in the new culture.

However, culture, when viewed through a Christian lens, is not an enemy to be feared, but a space to witness Christ. The Apostle Paul reminds us in 1 Corinthians 9:22, "I have become all things to all people so that by all possible means I might save some". This does not mean losing our identity in Christ but becoming flexible, sensitive and adaptable in order to reflect Jesus more effectively.

Some Therapeutic and Spiritual Principles to guide Families during Cultural Transitions

1. **Stay Rooted in Christ:** No matter how unfamiliar the environment, your family's foundation must remain in Christ. Encourage and go big on spiritual disciplines: such as prayer and fasting, meditating on scripture, worship; both individually and as a family. Build your Family systems based on your Christian values and how you desire to show up in this world, communicate it to all family members and revising it as the family evolves.

2. **Clarify Family Identity:** For example, you can say my family would like to show up as Trailblazers to our world; Becoming a trailblazer family means being a pioneering, purpose-driven household that sets positive examples, challenges societal norms "when necessary" and actively shapes a legacy.

It's about choosing intentional living over passive existence. You can see a detailed roadmap of a trailblazer family on our website: www.mothersofliving.co.uk

3. **Acknowledge Grief and Change:** Culture shift involves loss; loss of familiarity, customs, language, or status. Validate your family's feelings and circumstances.

Children may grieve differently and need emotional space to express confusion or fear. There should be openness for the children to express themselves; they can also speak to a trusted adult. This will help them and the parents to understand how they are processing the change around them. Parent can also follow up on members of the family on their feelings during any transition. In a similar case, I worked with a White British missionary family returning to the UK after years in West Africa. Their children, deeply shaped by Ghanaian culture, now found themselves teased at school for their accent, dress sense, and mannerisms. One child said, "It's like I don't belong here or there." As a therapist, I encouraged the parents to frame their children's cultural duality not as confusion, but as a gift. They began hosting Multicultural Ghanaian evenings at church and School inviting their UK friends to learn local dances and meals. This not only honoured their children's identity but helped them feel more confident within the recent community.

4. **Encourage Healthy Curiosity:** Immersion requires intentionality. Attend local events, ask questions without fear of appearing ignorant. Allow your children to share their curiosity, even if it leads to awkward moments. For example: one Christian family shared how their young son, after moving to a predominantly Asian community, asked loudly in Tesco (a grocery shop in the UK) why "the lady had dots on her head." Instead of shushing him, the parents used the moment to explain with respect; and later, invited their neighbour over to learn more. That child now speaks with confidence about different faiths and cultures because his parents modelled curiosity over shame. The Scripture teaches us that" there is neither Jew nor Gentile... for you are all one in Christ Jesus" (Galatians3:28). Cultural immersion is not about erasing differences; it's about seeing them through the lens of unity in Christ. It is choosing to love like Christ did, eating with outsiders, touching the untouchable, and listening without judgment.

Instead of approaching new ways of life with fear, foster a respectful curiosity, teach children to ask, "What is the purpose of this? How does it bring glory to God and blessing to humanity? What can we learn here? Does it work for us and our beliefs? How can we still be salt and light?"

5. **Build Bridges, Not Barriers:** Seek relationships within the new culture. Community offers protection against isolation. Show hospitality, just as Christ welcomed all. You can volunteer to be involve in community activities; this can open you to knowing the community. For example, there are so many communities to explore–online and onsite; Unique Women & Men Platform, Sunshine's club, Scout, Girls guide. Remember, you have been given access to enter the gate of your community because God trust you to take over the city for Jesus! You are the salt and light of the world." Matthew 5:13-15."Whoever wants a friend must first show themselves friendly. "Proverbs 18:34".

6. **Preserve and Integrate Values:** You don't have to abandon your God-given culture. Instead, prayerfully discern which values to retain, which to challenge, and

which new ones align with Kingdom principles. This is vital and should be communicated to members of the family (establish your Family Kingdom Principle. This is how culture is formed in families and societies).

7. **Open Dialogue:** At times, a child might be unusually quiet which may suggest they are experiencing something. Create space at home for regular reflection, ask your children what they're noticing, feeling, and learning at a meal table, leisure time or a relaxing atmosphere. Model vulnerability and hope; with gratitude, encouraging one another in the Word of God.

Therapeutically, I support families to process culture shock, reduce identity confusion, and foster open dialogue. To families immersed in new cultures, be patient with yourselves, your children may wrestle with identity, you may feel misunderstood, but do not give up. Keep listening, keep learning and keep leaning on grace. When you walk in love, humility and intentionality with purpose in mind, you won't just survive change; you will thrive within it. The goal isn't to lose your identity, but to expand it with grace; by this you're cultivating Kingdom culture.

Finally, remember that we are citizens of heaven first (Philippians 3: 20). Any earthly culture is temporary, and we are ambassadors of a greater Kingdom. As you immerse yourself in a new way of life, let it be an opportunity to deepen your family's spiritual maturity, expand your compassion, and embody the Gospel more fully. You are not alone; God goes before you, walks beside you, and lives within you.

Many blessings to you and your family.

About the Author

Lola Vincentia King is a Child and Family Therapist with a background in law and a Master's degree in Psychotherapy. With over five years of experience, she supports families navigating identity, trauma, and life transitions.

Lola leads *Sunshine's Club*, an online Bible club for children, and mentors young people on mental health and purpose discovery, championing faith and emotional well-being across society.

.

CHAPTER 16

NEAR-DEATH EXPERIENCE

What is Near-Death Experience

A near-death experience varies for each individual. It may occur as a sudden, life-altering event that changes one's perspective. Near-death experiences often bring about profound transformations, which can have either positive or negative effects on the individual, their family, and their outlook on life.

An NTD experience may linger for a long time, sometimes leaving a lifelong story to be shared repeatedly or concealed forever. It can have mental, spiritual, emotional, and physical impacts, individually or as a combination. These impacts may lead to lifestyle changes that are either beneficial or detrimental.

Many individuals who have had an NTD experience report that it leaves a lasting imprint, changing their outlook on life. Some are driven to seek answers to the questions raised by their experiences, while others turn to spiritual, medical, or lifestyle changes to cope.

In this piece, I will share my personal NTD experience, its profound impact on my faith in God, and the lifestyle changes it brought about. This experience has left me with a story I feel compelled to share repeatedly to testify to its significance and the lessons it taught me.

What brings about an NTD Experience?

A near-death experience can occur for various reasons and is a reality that can happen in anyone's life. It may be a one-off event or a recurring situation. However, it is crucial to learn the lessons the experience teaches and recognize the blessings it may bring.

Below are a few common questions individuals ask themselves during an NTD experience:

- Why me?
- What have I done wrong?

- What should I have done differently?
- What have I failed to do that I should have done?

These questions often remain unanswered, leaving individuals feeling frustrated and sad. While the reasons behind an NTD experience may remain unknown, it is essential to reflect on the lessons learned during such a profound encounter.

My NTD Experience

A near-death experience typically occurs during life-threatening situations, such as cardiac arrest, a brain haemorrhage, cancer, or other critical illnesses. In my case, a chronic disease threatened my life in 2018, leaving an indelible mark and a story worth sharing.

Near-death experiences are triggered during singular life-threatening episodes. In my case, a chronic disease threatened my life, and the impact has left a mark on my life and a story to be told over and over again.

The experience changed my perspective on life. It confirmed the mercy and faithfulness of God and reinforced the truth of His promises. As stated in **Lamentations 3:22-23:** *"It is of the Lord's mercies that we are not consumed because His compassions fail not. They are new every morning: great is Thy faithfulness."*

Seeking and Resting on God's Promises During an NTD Experience.

As the saying goes, "A problem shared is a problem halved." My husband and I decided to share our challenges with select friends and family members to request their support in prayer. Although these meetings often brought tears, fears, and emotional breakdowns, they also brought hope and the reassurance that God was in control.

Through corporate prayers and quiet moments with God, I drew strength from His Word. One scripture that brought me comfort was 1 Corinthians 10:13: *"There hath no temptation taken you, but such as is common to man: but God is faithful, who will not suffer you to be tempted above that ye are able; but will with the temptation also make a way to escape, that ye may be able to bear it."*

Hospital visits, tests, and examinations were frequent,

and the anxiety was overwhelming. Yet, I clung to God's promises, believing that the same God who delivered Daniel from the lions' den and Shadrach, Meshach, and Abednego from the fiery furnace would provide for me. Indeed, He did! Hallelujah!!

2 Timothy 4:18: *"And the Lord shall deliver me from every evil work and will preserve me unto His heavenly kingdom: to whom be glory forever and ever."*

The Impact of My NTD Experience on My Family

One of my children shared their perspective on my NTD experience. They described the initial shock and fear they felt upon learning about my illness. However, they also witnessed my unwavering faith and peace in the face of adversity, which left a lasting impression on them.

Here's an account of one of my children:

"I will never forget the day I found out my mum had a 'Near Death Experience." My dad told us we had a family meeting a few days prior and needed to travel from various locations. This was unusual, as he would typically share announcements in the WhatsApp family group chat. However, this time, he said it was "too important" for us not to be there in person. From this, I began to suspect they might be telling us they were moving to Nigeria or planning to be away for a while—but this was not the case.

When the moment arrived, everyone was laughing and relaxed, but my dad's seriousness eventually caught the room's attention. He spoke for a while, perhaps to soften the blow, but honestly, the only thing I remember is the tears rolling down his face as he told us my mother had cancer and had been quietly attending treatments in the mornings. I froze instantly. It was as if my entire body had been seized by fear and shock. My mother, whom I had always seen as a mighty superhero, now faced something that could take her away from us.

I had never seen my dad cry, except maybe once or twice at a funeral. But this time was different—I saw my dad scared and overwhelmed by a situation he couldn't control. The same emotions gripped the room. My older brother, Daniel, fell to his knees, screaming "No," as if he had just heard she was gone. Others began throwing out panicked and angry questions: why were we only finding out now? How bad was it? Meanwhile, some, like me, just sat there and wept, unable to produce any other response or sound.

Amidst the fear and sadness, I witnessed the most remarkable thing I have ever seen. My mum, the very person enduring this pain, the one who should have been most upset or worried, sat there peacefully, a serene smile on her face. She remained completely calm, filled with the Holy Spirit, and told us, "God is in control" and "Keep your faith." I couldn't believe it. The person who was wounded was tending to everyone else in the room—comforting my dad and encouraging my siblings. That was when I realised this woman had indeed encountered Jesus. Only someone who has met the Messiah, who rose from the dead, could have such peace in a storm.

My mum's relentless faith didn't stop there. Later, I went to my room for the first time, and she came in to pray with me. Her faith and hope in God imparted something spiritual to me. Through this situation, the lukewarm Christian I was—who barely spoke to God—suddenly put all his faith and trust in Him. Seeing my mum's unwavering belief, I knew it had to be authentic.

The journey wasn't easy. The months that followed were filled with tears and fear as I grappled with the possibility of losing my best friend. But daily, my mum encouraged me. I saw her walk-in grace and strength as though there were no battles. When others worried about her, she eased their minds, constantly reminding us, "Don't forget the God we serve." Her faith and love for God inspired me deeply. Even if she hadn't made it, I would still know a God in heaven who hears our cries and binds our wounds. My mum showed no fear, and even if she felt it, her faith in Jesus consistently overpowered her emotions. Indeed, she was a woman held by God. She didn't just display pure faith that I will always hold onto—she demonstrated that even in life's darkest, lowest moments, when our backs are against the wall, God will make a way.

Who is this mighty woman of valour? She is merely a child of God. She showed me that her faith was the standard we should all strive for. She wasn't better than anyone else in our family—she believed in the words we all read.

To conclude, my mother is a child who never stops depending on her Father and has a heart that never forgets Christ. Through this, she brings warmth and inspiration to everyone she meets."

The Impact of a Near-Death (NTD) Experience on My Faith

In **2 Corinthians 7:11, t**he Bible says, "*What carefulness it wrought in you, yea, what clearing of yourselves, yea, what indignation, yea, what fear, yea, what vehement (intense) desire, yea, what zeal, yea, what revenge!*"

This verse describes the positive results of godly sorrow, which aligns with God's will and purpose. It represents a transformative experience that leads to repentance and spiritual growth. In this case, the Corinthians' godly sorrow prompted a profound change, demonstrating the power of repentance.

The diagnosis brought with it great fear and anger toward me. I questioned: What have I done that I shouldn't have? It left me in great carefulness, taking extra precautions, thirsting to make things right again, yearning to undo what had been done, and desiring intensely to turn back time. I felt driven to find answers to my many unanswered questions, and I longed for change. If the devil was indeed behind this affliction, I sought an opportunity for revenge against him.

The experience left me with sleepless nights, gazing toward heaven, asking God for divine intervention and mercy, not only for me but also for my entire household. It was a time of deep self-examination and reflection, a season of emptying myself before God.

I must admit, there were moments when I could not pray. Often, I would lie down in silence, unable to articulate my thoughts or phrase my prayers. I usually felt overwhelmed—emotional, sorrowful, perplexed, and hopeless—yet I poured out my heart to God, my Maker.

As the scripture says in **2 Corinthians 7:11**: *"Just look what God has done by making you feel sorry! You sincerely want to prove you are innocent. You are angry. You are shocked. You are eager to see that justice is done. You want to be in right standing before God, deserving of a second chance as you plead for His mercy."*

In **Hebrews 2:15**, the Bible also states, "*And deliver them who through fear of death were all their lifetime subject to bondage.*"

This verse reminds us that the fear of death is a universal human condition that binds and oppresses. Similarly, sin enslaves anyone who has not yet accepted the Lord's freedom. But thanks be to God, who delivers us from the fear of death and grants us glorious hope, which allows us to anticipate the eternal glory He has reserved for us (2 Corinthians 4:18).

Divine Intervention in My Near-Death Experience

My near-death experience did not come with many signs or symptoms except for noticeable weight loss. I lacked appetite, and the sight of food repelled me. I was deeply distressed and unhappy. My husband often pleaded with me to eat, even just a little, but his efforts were in vain.

Day and night, I called upon the Lord to intervene and have mercy on me. I clung to faith, believing that divine intervention would come, though I didn't know how. I refused most of the treatments offered by the hospital, affirming to the medical team that my faith was in God for healing. I trusted that He would not fail me.

I stood firm on the Word of God in 2 Corinthians 4:8-18: *"We are troubled on every side, yet not distressed; we are perplexed, but not in despair; persecuted, but not forsaken; cast down, but not destroyed..."*

10 Always bearing about in the body the dying of the Lord Jesus, the life of Jesus might manifest in our body.

11 For we which live are always delivered unto death for Jesus'
sake, that the life of Jesus might be made manifest in our mortal
flesh. 12 So then death worketh in us, but life in you. 13 We have
the same spirit of faith, according as it is written, I believed, and
therefore have I spoken; we also believe, and therefore speak;
14 Knowing that he which raised the Lord Jesus shall raise us
also by Jesus and shall present us with you.

15 For all things are for your sakes, that the abundant grace
might through the thanksgiving of many redound to the glory
of God. 16 For this cause, we faint not; but though our outward
man perishes, the inward man is renewed daily.

17 For our light affliction, which is but for a moment, worketh
for us a far more exceeding and eternal weight of glory; 18 While
we look not at the things which are seen, but at the things which
are not seen: for the things which are seen are temporal; but
the things which are not seen are eternal.

Lessons Learned from My NTD Experience

Lessons from such an experience can vary for each individual. It's essential to reflect and ponder what God might be teaching us. For me, one key lesson has been the value of journaling. I now count my blessings and name them individually, writing them down for future reference so I can continually appreciate God's faithfulness.

I have learned that God is faithful and always has our best interests at heart, even when He allows us to face trials. He hears our prayers and the prayers of others. My experience affirmed that He truly is a good God.

Another profound lesson is the power of collective or corporate prayer. I shared my struggles with fellow faith believers, who prayerfully rallied around me. This aligns with **James 5:13-15**:" *Is any among you afflicted? Let him pray. Is any merry? Let him sing psalms. Is anyone sick among you? Let him call for the church's elders, and let them pray over him, anointing him with oil in the name of the Lord. And the prayer of faith shall save the sick, and the Lord shall raise him." I also learned that God could use our experiences to get our attention. Just as He spoke to Moses through a burning bush* *that wasn't consumed, He often uses trials to draw us closer to Him. He promises in Isaiah 43:2 that it will not consume us when we pass through the fire. Let us trust that He is with us all the way.*

A Message for Anyone Facing an NTD Experience

The message is simple: "Have faith in God." Where God sees faith, He will indeed honour it. Do not go through such an experience alone. Call upon the church, seek godly counsel, and surround yourself with believers who can join their faith with yours.

As 2 Thessalonians 3:3 says*:" But the Lord is faithful, who shall establish you and keep you from evil."*

And 2 Timothy 4:18 reminds us: "And the Lord shall deliver me from every evil work and will preserve me unto His heavenly kingdom: to whom be glory forever and ever."

Amen.

I have learned that God is faithful and always has our best interests at heart, even when He allows us to face trials.

About the Author

Florence Olujoke Peters has faithfully followed God since her salvation in 1981. She's a devoted wife, mentor, and teacher who's seen God's miracles in her life. Florence is active in the marketplace ministry, sharing Christ's love in everyday spaces.

In 2020, she launched *Mothers of the Mighty*, a global movement uniting Christian women to pray for children and youth. With a servant's heart and passion for intercession, Florence seeks to serve others and glorify God. She's blessed with six children and two grandchildren, and her ministry impacts lives in South London and beyond, fostering fellowship and support.

CHAPTER 17

YOUR ATTITUDE TOWARDS LIFE DETERMINES YOUR DESTINY

Your attitude is not just a reaction to circumstances; it is the creative force that shapes your future and carves out the success you aspire to achieve. Your attitude toward life serves as the compass that guides your destiny. John C. Maxwell brilliantly captures this when he states, "You are only an attitude away from success."

This idea emphasises that a positive mindset can illuminate even the darkest paths, transforming setbacks into stepping stones. When you maintain optimism, you empower yourself to navigate challenges with grace and resilience. A positive attitude nurtures resilience, allowing us to recover from setbacks and perceive obstacles as opportunities for growth.

Our attitude toward life plays a vital role in shaping our destinies. It can influence how we interact with others, look at life's challenges, and make choices. When we approach life with optimism, we are more likely to take risks, pursue our passions, and engage in relationships that contribute to a meaningful and fulfilling life.

On the other hand, a negative attitude can create a self-fulfilling prophecy. If we continuously focus on the negative aspects of situations, we may overlook opportunities and find ourselves trapped in a cycle of pessimism. This mindset can lead to a lack of motivation and a diminished sense of purpose, ultimately directing our lives in a direction that may not align with our true desires.

A biblical story that illustrates how our attitudes can shape our destinies for good is the tale of Joseph. Despite being sold into slavery by his brothers and facing numerous hardships, Joseph maintained a positive attitude and faith in God. His resilience and ability to interpret dreams ultimately led him to become an influential leader in Egypt, saving many lives from famine. Joseph's story demonstrates how a positive outlook and trust in a higher purpose can result in extraordinary outcomes, regardless of circumstances.

Another example is David, who faced Goliath. While others viewed Goliath as an insurmountable obstacle, David's faith and positive mindset empowered him to confront and overcome what seemed impossible. This narrative reinforces the idea that our attitudes can shape our destinies for the better.

My journey into studying pharmacy at 40, while being a wife and mother of three young children, my youngest just over a year old, is a powerful testament to how attitude can shape destiny. Childcare is one of the biggest challenges faced by families with young children in developed countries.

Transitioning from a computer science background to a different field required immense courage, faith, and determination. I made the bold decision to pursue pharmacy despite the challenges of balancing family responsibilities and educational demands. This experience shows that it is never too late to chase one's dreams.

Some of my most cherished Bible verses during this journey were Proverbs 3:5-6 “Trust in the Lord with all your heart and lean not on your understanding; in all your ways submit to him, and he will direct your path,” and Philippians 4:13 “I can do all things through Christ who strengthens me.” Like the biblical figures who faced daunting obstacles, my story illustrates how a strong mindset can lead to significant achievements. I maintained my faith through adversity, embracing the challenge of returning to school.

This journey sets a powerful example for my children and demonstrates that redefining one’s path at any stage in life is possible. I hope my experience inspires those who may feel constrained by their current circumstances, showing that a positive attitude and a willingness to adapt can lead to new opportunities.

I embody the message that my destiny is not solely determined by past choices or age, but by my choices today and the attitudes I adopt. My journey reminds me that I can create a fulfilling future with determination and belief in myself.

In conclusion, our attitudes serve as a lens through which we view the world and our place within it. By consciously adopting a positive attitude, we enhance our life experiences and inspire those around us.

This ripple effect can lead to a more supportive environment, fostering collaboration and shared success.

About the Author

Funmi Ifabua is a woman of faith, a practising pharmacist, an entrepreneur and a devoted mother. Her passion lies in bringing both physical and spiritual healing to those who are struggling.

She loves praying with fellow believers and finds great joy in supporting and encouraging others—especially women and young people—to never give up.

Funmi believes that, with faith in God and grit, anyone can overcome life's challenges and walk boldly in their God-given purpose.

CHAPTER 18

COLLABORATION

Living the Divine Design Together

Across every season of life, we are bound by a shared journey. Over the past two decades or more, I've had the extraordinary privilege of walking alongside women from all backgrounds. Together, we've experienced laughter and lament, triumphs and trials.

Through it all, one enduring truth has stood tall: we are better together. There is unmatched power in connection, purpose in unity, and profound beauty in collaboration, and that is the truth!

What Is Collaboration?

At its core, collaboration is the act of working with others, combining our unique strengths, perspectives, and gifts to achieve a goal greater than any of us could accomplish alone. It is not just a workplace strategy or a popular buzzword. Instead, it is a deeply spiritual and profoundly human practice—woven into the fabric of our being by the very One who created us.

To truly understand collaboration, we must begin with God Himself—the ultimate model of unity. From the beginning, the Trinity—Father, Son, and Holy Spirit—has existed in perfect collaboration. Each Person is distinct, yet working in seamless harmony.

In Genesis, God declares, *"It is not good for the man to be alone"* (Genesis 2:18). This was not only a statement about marriage, but a foundational truth about human design. We are made for relationships, for connection, for community, for shared purpose.

In 1 Corinthians 12, the apostle Paul paints a vivid picture of this design using the metaphor of the body: *"Though the body is made up of many parts, it forms one body. So it is with Christ."* Each member—whether hand, foot, eye, or ear—has a vital role. No part is unnecessary. No part can say, "I don't need you." What a profound vision of collaborative living!

Collaboration as a Spiritual Calling

From a Christian perspective, collaboration is not just beneficial; it is essential. It is how we live out Jesus' command to love one another, how we bear each other's burdens, and how we use our God-given gifts for the common good.

Collaboration requires:

- **Humility** - recognizing we don't have all the answers.
- **Generosity** - sharing our time, knowledge, and resources.
- **Faith** - trusting that together, with God's help, we can do immeasurably more than we imagine.

In practicing collaboration, we reflect God's nature and participate in His redemptive work in the world.

Collaboration in the Professional World

Whether you're leading a team, managing a household, serving in ministry, or navigating community life, the ability to collaborate effectively is a critical skill. When we bring our gifts together in a spirit of cooperation, we unlock tremendous potential. A team of similar thinkers may reach quick consensus, but diversity brings depth. Different backgrounds, skills, and ways of thinking form a rich tapestry of ideas. When these are welcomed and woven together, innovation blossoms.

Trying to carry the load alone leads to exhaustion. Collaboration lightens the burden. Each person brings their strengths, and together we accomplish more efficiently, sustainably, and joyfully. Innovation often emerges not from isolated effort but from dynamic exchanges. Brainstorming, discussion, and shared imagination spark new ideas. Collaboration is fertile ground for creativity. Collaboration builds trust and respect. It fosters clear communication, active listening, and shared accountability. In such an environment, people thrive—not just professionally, but personally.

Practicing Collaborative Living

How do we nurture a lifestyle of collaboration? Here are practical, faith-rooted steps:

Cultivate Humility: Philippians 2:3 reminds us, *"Do nothing out of selfish ambition... Rather, in humility value others above yourselves."* Approach every team, partnership, and conversation with a learner's heart.

Listen to Understand: True listening requires presence. Set aside distractions. Seek to understand, not just to respond. Respectful listening builds trust and deepens connection.

Communicate with clarity: Say what you mean, and say it with grace. Clear communication avoids confusion. Respectful words create safety and foster cooperation.

Honor Each Person's Strength: Everyone brings something unique. Recognize the talents in those around you, and invite people to shine in their strengths.

Be Generous with what you know: Share insights, tools, and encouragement freely. Collaboration thrives where generosity is the norm.

Unify Around a Shared Vision: Great teams know where they're headed. Align on purpose. Revisit the "why" often to stay connected and inspired.

Handle Conflict with Grace

Handle Conflict with Grace: Disagreement is inevitable, but it doesn't have to be divisive. Face conflict with honesty, focus on solutions, and seek peace. As Romans 12:18 encourages, *"If it is possible... live at peace with everyone."*

Celebrate Together: Acknowledge milestones, express gratitude, and celebrate wins. Recognition strengthens morale and reinforces a collaborative spirit. Do you realise that this book is a collaborative work? We need to celebrate this great achievement together. It has been a joint effort, and worthy of celebration indeed!

Pray Together: In faith-centred spaces, prayer unites hearts and aligns efforts with God's will. It reminds us that we are not alone in our work. So it is very important to pray together.

A Life Transformed by Collaboration

Imagine the possibilities: homes where spouses and children share responsibilities and support each other's dreams; workplaces where trust replaces competition and diversity is celebrated; churches where every gift is appreciated and used to honor God; communities where people unite across differences to address needs and foster hope.

So, wherever you are in life, whether you are starting a new business, a new career, leading a team, raising a family, or entering a new season, the call to collaboration is for you. Let us live as people of unity. Let us listen, serve, and build together. Let us be the hands and feet of Christ in a world longing for healing and hope. Because when we collaborate, we not only achieve more, we become more. We fulfil the beautiful purpose for which we were created.

Together, we are truly better.

About the Author

Oyinlola Bukky Akande (OBA) is a life coach, speaker, and publisher with over 25 years of retail and sales experience. She's a customer service expert and is the author of books like *'Diary of the Unique Woman', The Life Wires' Coupons', 'Hello, I'm Pleased To Meet You'* and *'Go Selfless'*. Some of the anthologies she has co-authored are *'Unique Insights', 'Unique Foresights'* and *'Treasured'*.

As President of *Unique Women International*, OBA empowers women and young professionals through mentorship, guidance, and networking opportunities.

PART THREE

REVEAL

CHAPTER 19

APPRECIATE LIFE MORE

If there's anything that life has taught us, it's that the life you have is not truly yours. It's a borrowed life, a gift from the divine, so you need to appreciate it. Not everyone born will live to a full and ripe old age.

Since my near-death experience in December 2005, the Lord delivered me and granted me a new lease on life. I have come to appreciate God and life more deeply. I became gravely ill as a consequence of chemotherapy, and I nearly died. The chemotherapy and all treatments were entirely halted by the specialist team caring for me. Thank God, who did not allow the enemies and sickness to prevail over me.

My testimony is that we took the situation to God in prayer

after the treatment was stopped, and God intervened, giving me a clean bill of health and delivering me from high-grade cancer. Glory to God El-Shaddai and Jehovah Rophe for His faithfulness as a specialist combatant. These two scriptures always come to mind:

"If it had not been the Lord who was on our side," let Israel now say, "If it had not been the Lord who was on our side when men rose against us, then they would have [quickly] swallowed us alive when their wrath was kindled against us; then the waters would have engulfed us, the torrent would have swept over our soul;" **Psalms 124:1-4 AMP.**

"Then the raging waters would have swept over our soul." Blessed be the Lord, who has not given us as prey to be torn by their teeth. We have escaped like a bird from the snare of the fowlers; the trap is broken, and we have escaped." **Psalms 124:5 7** AMP.

Psalms 90:12 says, *"So teach us to number our days, that we may apply our hearts unto wisdom."*

The wisdom lies in understanding that, as human beings,

we should recognize the brevity of life and make our lives count, for our lives matter greatly both in this reality and eternity with God.

Appreciating Life More: A Peek into Scripture

Life is a precious gift, filled with countless opportunities for joy, growth, and purpose. Yet, amidst the busyness of our daily routines, many overlook the beauty of existence and fail to appreciate our blessings. By turning to Scripture, we find guidance and inspiration to live with gratitude, mindfulness, and a heart whole of appreciation for the life God has given us.

Recognising Life as a Gift

The Bible emphasizes that life itself is a divine gift. **In Psalm 139:14**, David declares, *"I praise you because I am fearfully and wonderfully made; your works are wonderful, I know that full well."*

This verse reminds us that our existence is a testament to God's intricate craftsmanship. Every heartbeat, breath, and moment reflects His intentional design.

Similarly, in **James 1:17,** we are reminded, *"Every good and perfect gift is from above, coming down from the Father of the heavenly lights, who does not change like shifting shadows."* Life is one of these perfect gifts with all its joys and challenges.

Recognizing this truth invites us to approach each day with reverence and gratitude. While we often focus on the bigger things, such as our careers, education, and relationships, if we take the time to step back and appreciate the little things in life, we can truly be blessed. God created us with many unique gifts and blessings that are often overlooked or taken for granted. The small moments of joy from a beautiful sunset, a child's laughter, a hug from a friend or family member, or even a quiet moment of reflection are all valid reasons to pause and appreciate what God has given us. The world is teeming with beauty and abundance if we take the time to look for it.

We should take moments to savour something simple, like watching a flower bloom or listening to birds chirping. Acknowledging small victories that add up over time is essential, such as completing a project at work or learning something new. These moments deserve to be cherished and celebrated! The truth is that life is short, and every moment matters.

Don't let essential moments go unnoticed because you're too busy focusing on "bigger" things. Take the time to recognise all the beauty around you – even if those moments are small. Do this regularly, and your life will become more meaningful and purposeful. After all, these little things make up your life story! God has given us so much abundance in our lives – let's not forget to be grateful for it! Try each day to appreciate the little things in life – they can add up over time! Taking the time to enjoy these small moments can give you peace of mind and help you live a more blessed life. The scriptures are a guide to the truth that life is to be appreciated–Luke 16:19, Psalms 9:1, 1 Thessalonians **5:18, Psalms 106:1, Psalms 118:1.**

Finding Joy in the Present

Modern life often distracts us with worries about the future or regrets about the past, causing us to miss the present moment. Yet, the Bible encourages us to embrace the here and now. In **Ecclesiastes 3:12-13,** Solomon writes, *"I know* *that there is nothing better for people than to be happy and to do good while they live. Each of them may eat and drink and find satisfaction in all their toil—this is the gift of God."*

The scripture above calls us to find joy in simple pleasures—sharing a meal, engaging in meaningful work, and enjoying relationships. By focusing on these blessings, we cultivate a deeper appreciation for the present.

Gratitude in All Circumstances

Appreciating life doesn't mean ignoring difficulties or pretending pain doesn't exist. Instead, it involves acknowledging that there are reasons to be grateful even in challenges. **1 Thessalonians 5:16-18** advises, *"Rejoice always, pray continually, give thanks in all circumstances; for this is God's will for you in Christ Jesus."*

This attitude of gratitude transforms our perspective. Instead of dwelling on what we lack, we see God's provision in every situation. Trials become growth opportunities, and moments of pain remind us of God's sustaining grace.

Stewardship of Life

Appreciating life also involves living responsibly and purposefully. In **Ephesians 5:15-16**, Paul writes, *"Be very careful, then, how you live—not as unwise but as wise, making the most of every opportunity, because the days are evil."* This scripture urges us to be mindful stewards of our time and resources, using them to glorify God and serve others. Jesus Himself modelled this principle in John 10:10b, saying, "I have come that they may have life, and have it to the full." To truly appreciate life, we must embrace Jesus's abundant life—one marked by love, service, and a deep connection with God.

Trusting God's Plan

Finally, appreciating life means trusting God's plan, even when we don't understand it. **Jeremiah 29:11** assures us, *"For I know the plans I have for you," declares the Lord, "plans to prosper you and not to harm you, plans to give you hope and a future."* By trusting in God's sovereignty, we can approach each day with confidence and gratitude, knowing He is working all things for our good.

WE NEED TO APPRECIATE LIFE MORE–By being present, cultivating gratitude, and pursuing our passions, we can appreciate and experience life to the fullest, both now and in the future. We do not want to ignore or move on from complex thoughts or feelings. Instead, we can choose to go through them to build emotional resilience.

How do You Appreciate Life More?

Be thankful for what DIDN'T happen -No matter how bad things are, they could almost always be worse." This may seem silly, but it can improve your mood if you start noticing the things that didn't go wrong.

Don't hold on to your anger or hurt–You can't be upset and grateful simultaneously, and life is too short to look for reasons to be upset." Holding a grudge or focusing on a perceived slight never does anyone any good, especially you, the person holding on. Is it a big deal in the grand scheme of things anyway? Take a deep breath... and let it go. You'll be doing yourself a favour!

Savor life's little moments—When you remember those moments that brought joy to your heart and a smile, you will realize that life is to be cherished, like the joy of a new baby in the house and the baby taking the first steps... Appreciate those little things!

Express your gratitude by living it–There are many things to be grateful for. Let it be shown in your attitude that you're indeed thankful. Express it always

Give—When you give to others, you may not immediately realise how much your life can impact them.

- Mindfulness–Sit with your feelings and your thoughts.
- Love Yourself.
- Hyperfocus on the Positive.
- Make a Gratitude List.
- Take a Break.
- Celebrate Your Wins.
- Stay Thankful.

Showing appreciation for the good things in your life and expressing gratitude for the people in your life will always pay excellent dividends back into your own life!

Likewise, appreciating life and being grateful ADD VALUE TO YOUR LIFE.

There are 8 ways to add value to your life:

- Mindfulness. Take a moment to relax.
- Follow your Passion. Make sure you're doing what you love.
- Self-Care. Treat yourself well, feel beautiful, be assertive.
- Be Self-Aware.
- Simplify your Life. Don't be too hard on yourself.
- Have Daily Goals.
- Live a Healthy Lifestyle. Diet and exercise.
- Be Open to Change. It brings transformation.

There are Practical Ways to Appreciate Life More

Start Each Day with Gratitude: When you wake up, reflect on one thing you are thankful for.

Spend Time in Nature: Admire God's creation, as encouraged in Psalm 19:1, which says, "The heavens declare the glory of God; the skies proclaim the work of his hands."

Serve Others: Kindness reminds us of the joy of giving.
Pause and Reflect: Take moments throughout your day

to pray, meditate, or breathe deeply, focusing on God's blessings.

End the Day with Thanksgiving: Before sleeping, thank God for the experiences, lessons, and moments.
Be grateful for little things, always

Conclusion

Appreciating life more is an emotional exercise, and a spiritual practice rooted in Scripture. We can live with a profound sense of thankfulness and purpose by recognising life as a divine gift, finding joy in the present, expressing gratitude in all circumstances, stewarding our lives wisely, and trusting God's plan. Let us take to heart the words of **Psalm 118:24:** *"This is the day the Lord has made; let us rejoice and be glad in it."* Indeed, every day is a reason to celebrate and appreciate the beautiful gift of life thrown at us by the creator of the universe.

Psalms 103:1/5 talks about appreciating the good life we have all received from the Lord and being grateful to Him always.

"Bless the Lord, O my soul: and all within me, bless his holy name. Bless the Lord, O my soul, and forget not all his benefits: who forgives all thine iniquities; who healeth all thy diseases; who redeemed thy life from destruction; who crowned thee with loving-kindness and tender mercies; who satisfied thy mouth with good things; so that thy youth is renewed like the eagle's." **Psalm 103:1-5 KJV**

Only God can gift you the blessings of Redemption, forgiveness, Love, kindness, healing, satisfaction, and renewal of strength so you're sustained on this side of eternity.

Remember, it's only one life. Live it purposefully today. Tomorrow is not promised, and in whatever situation you may be in, appreciate this life more...

DON'T YOU EVER FORGET OR TAKE FOR GRANTED THE GIFT OF LIFE.

The happiest people are the people who appreciate and value what they have right now because when you value what you have, it values you and your life.

YOUR LIFE IS VALUABLE… Appreciate it. The words in Jim Reeves's song lyrics echo on;

This world is not my own; I'm just passing through…

Bible References

Psalms 90:5/6,9 NKJV

"You carry them away like a flood; They are like a sleep. In the morning, they are like grass that grows up: In the morning, it flourishes and grows up; In the evening, it is cut down and withers.

9 For all our days have passed away in Your wrath; We finish our years like a sigh."

Psalm 103:15/16 NKJV

"As for man, his days are like grass; As a flower of the field, so he flourishes. For the wind passes over it, and it is gone, and its place remembers it no more."

About the Author

Adenike Aiyeola is a retired health practitioner with 35 years of experience. She has a multifaceted portfolio in health, community impact, and faith. Adenike is passionate about reading, supporting, and empowering individuals, especially women. Her journey showcases resilience, strategic vision, and unwavering faith.

She serves as an inspiration and beacon of possibility for women seeking to reach their next level. Through her experiences and passion, Adenike empowers others to step into their potential and make a positive impact. Her dedication to empowering women is a testament to her commitment to creating lasting change.

CHAPTER 20

GAINING VALUABLE EXPERIENCE AS AN EYE-OPENER

"Experience is not the best teacher; evaluated experience is the best teacher," says John C. Maxwell. 2 Corinthians 1:4 (NLT) states, "He comforts us in all our troubles so that we can comfort others. When they are troubled, we can give them the same comfort God has given us."

Many years ago, a man in my community approached me for financial assistance. For some inexplicable reason, I agreed to take out a loan on his behalf. Unfortunately, the business he invested in with that loan failed, leaving me to repay it.

A few years after this incident, I encountered **Proverbs 6:1-3 (NLT**): *"My child, if you have put up security for a friend's debt or agreed to guarantee the debt of a stranger— [2] if you have trapped yourself by your agreement and are caught by what you said— [3] follow my advice and save yourself, for you have placed yourself at your friend's mercy. Now swallow your pride; beg to have your name erased."*

This passage warns against taking on another person's loan, as it can expose one to significant financial risk if they fail to pay.

This eye-opening experience has imparted a life lesson that has become my life's guiding principle and value.

- Evaluated experience is an influential teacher that transforms knowledge into wisdom, fosters self-awareness, enhances decision-making, builds resilience, and promotes continuous improvement.

- Evaluated experience means actively learning and growing from our experiences, not simply going through them.

Our text, 2 Corinthians 1:4, highlights the importance of shared experience. It begins by noting that God is the source of all comfort. He comforts us in our troubles, acknowledging that everyone faces difficulties, and that God is present and active during those times.

God's comfort is not just for our benefit; it's given to us "so that we can comfort others." This implies a responsibility to share the comfort we've received with those suffering.

The verse emphasizes delivering to others "the same comfort God has given us." This suggests that our experiences of hardship and our comfort from God prepare us to empathize with and minister to others undergoing similar trials. We can relate to their pain because we've been there. The shared experience could serve as a bridge.

This verse highlights how personal suffering, when met with God's comfort, can equip us for ministry and life journey. Our struggles become a source of strength and understanding that allows us to connect with and support others in their struggles.

The verse presents a powerful model of how God's grace and comfort in our lives can be channelled to bring healing and hope to others. It encourages believers to embrace their good and bad experiences, knowing that God can use them to shape us into instruments of His love and compassion.

Therefore, gaining valuable experience can be a profound "eye-opener" in several ways, leading to significant personal and professional growth.

Benefits of Evaluated Experience

- The evaluated experience motivates reality checks. Through reflection, we can consider the unpleasant truth about the situation rather than trying to ignore it.

- Evaluated experience shatters idealized notions or preconceived ideas. It reveals the practical realities of a problem or even life itself. This is a humbling but essential process, forcing one to adapt and become more realistic in one's expectations.

- Evaluated experience empowers self-discovery, which is invaluable for making informed decisions about the future. Facing real-world challenges and navigating different situations helps one to discover one's strengths, weaknesses, and passions. We learn what we are good at, what we enjoy, and what we need to improve on. Know thyself.

- Evaluated experience produces skill development. It allows us to put our knowledge into practice, hone our skills, and develop new ones. We learn by doing, making mistakes, and finding solutions to real problems.

- Evaluated experience develops perspective shifts. We broaden our perspective by encountering diverse people, cultures, and viewpoints.

- Evaluated expertise helps us understand different ways of thinking and living while fostering empathy and tolerance.

- Evaluating experiences boosts confidence. Whether positive or negative, each event contributes to our sense of self-efficacy and belief in our ability to handle future situations. Thus, successfully navigating challenges and overcoming obstacles builds confidence.

- Evaluated experience clarifies goals. By trying different activities and seeing what resonates with you, you can better understand what you want to achieve and what truly matters to you.

- Evaluated experience fosters adaptability and resilience. Life rarely goes according to plan. Evaluated experience teaches us to be adaptable, to roll with the punches, and to bounce back from setbacks. It builds resilience, essential for navigating life's ups and downs.

- Evaluated experience expands your network. Through evaluated experience, you meet new people, build relationships, and grow your network. These connections can open doors to future opportunities and provide valuable support and guidance.

- Evaluated experience creates a deeper understanding. It offers a more nuanced comprehension of concepts, ideas, and processes, moving you beyond theoretical knowledge to practical wisdom.

- Evaluated experience nurtures an appreciation for the journey. Even when challenging, gaining evaluated expertise can be incredibly rewarding. It fosters a sense of accomplishment and appreciation for personal growth and self-discovery.

- Evaluated experience involves experiencing things and actively reflecting on them to extract valuable lessons and insights.

- Evaluating experience transforms knowledge into wisdom. Knowledge is information; we can learn facts and theories from books or lectures. Experience is the application of that knowledge. Wisdom is understanding, and it is only through evaluating your experiences that you gain true wisdom—a profound grasp of why things happened, what you learned, and how to apply those lessons in the future.

- Evaluated experience fosters self-awareness. It helps you identify your strengths and weaknesses, allowing you to build on and address the latter. Reflecting on what resonated with you and what did not helps clarify your values and passions, guiding you toward a more fulfilling path. Understanding your reactions and responses in different situations promotes personal growth and development.

- Evaluated experience enhances decision-making. Analysing good and bad decisions helps you learn from your mistakes and make better choices in the future. By reviewing your experiences, you can start to recognize patterns. And trends that can inform your decision-making process. Evaluated expertise leads to improved judgment and the ability to anticipate potential outcomes.

- Evaluated experience builds Resilience. Reflecting on how you handled challenges and setbacks in the past can help you develop resilience and the ability to bounce back from future difficulties. Evaluating your emotional responses in different situations can help you learn to manage your emotions more effectively. Evaluating experiences reinforces a growth mindset, which involves believing that you can learn and grow from any situation..

- Evaluated experience promotes continuous improvement. Assessing your experiences helps you identify areas where you can improve your skills, knowledge, or approach. It encourages you to seek feedback from others and be open to constructive criticism. The evaluation process allows you to adapt your strategies and evolve as a person and professional.

How to Evaluate Your Experiences.

- Reflect: take time to reflect on your experiences, both positive and negative. What happened? How did you feel? What did you learn?

- Writing down your thoughts and reflections in a journal can help you process your experiences and gain deeper insights.

- Seek feedback and ask others for their perspectives on your performance or behaviour.

- Analyse the patterns; look for patterns in your experiences. What are your strengths? What areas do you need to work on?

- Apply the lessons learned. Use your insights from evaluating your experiences to make better decisions and improve your future performance.

About the Author

James Adeyemi is a passionate servant of God and a dedicated individual to others. As a mental health practitioner and certified coach, he empowers others to take charge of their growth. Recognised as an anointed minister with *RCCG*, he pastors *Impact Centre* in Bicester and leads *Global Impact*. James is a positive leader, sound in the Word, and dedicated to helping believers become purpose-driven individuals.

He inspires millions and joyfully shares his life with his wife, Pastor Mrs. Bukola, and their daughter, Ore. A prophetic edge marks his ministry, and he is committed to adding value to others.

Chapter 21

SEEING YOURSELF DIFFERENTLY

Overcoming the Littleness Syndrome

What do you see when you look in the mirror? Your features, right? Your shape, complexion, height, and even weight? But who you see in the mirror is not your complete reflection. When I was younger, I didn't like full-length mirrors; I didn't like who I saw in them. I used to see a lanky girl whose breasts seemed too close to her hips. I disliked myself because of one body part—my torso. I have a high waist, which makes me look disproportionate. The funny thing is, while I was busy obsessing over my short torso and complaining about it, others admired my long legs! You might also have something you don't like about yourself—the shape of your ears, the size of your nose, the arrangement of your teeth, or the colour of your eyes. But these features don't define who you indeed are.

However, the physical mirrors we use are the least of our problems. The real issue lies in those metaphorical mirrors that distort our self-concept, making us feel unworthy, insignificant, or incapable of achieving what we believe we are destined to do. It is the reflection in those mirrors that screams back at us, saying, "You are not enough," "You can't do this," and "You'll never succeed." This taunting can be debilitating, and if not challenged, it will prevent us from stepping into the fullness of our purpose. This is what I call the "Littleness Syndrome."

The actual issue lies in those metaphorical mirrors that distort our self-concept, making us feel unworthy, insignificant, or incapable of achieving what we believe we are destined to do.

The Power of Self-Perception

Allow me to challenge a widely held belief: although we live with ourselves and are closest to ourselves, we often think we know everything about who we are. However, this isn't entirely true. Being your constant companion and familiar with the 'real me' does not give you a complete understanding of yourself. In reality, many tend to lean toward one side or the other. Those who focus on their strengths may become arrogant and overlook areas for improvement, suffering from self-enhancement. Bias. While those who focus on their weaknesses magnify their faults and define themselves by past mistakes, they suffer from self-deprecation. This chapter is dedicated to those who undervalue themselves. I'm speaking to those with poor self-esteem who fail to recognise the divine worth and value within them. Maintaining this outlook leads to a less fulfilling existence.

In my book, From Little to Limitless, I define the Littleness Syndrome as a profoundly ingrained condition rooted in fear, insecurity, and a distorted sense of self that many individuals unknowingly carry. This mindset creates an invisible ceiling, preventing people from embracing the vast potential that God has instilled within them. It manifests as hesitation, self-doubt, and retreating from opportunities to grow, stretch, and thrive. The Littleness Syndrome is a mentality deeply rooted in fear, self-doubt, and negative self-perception. It convinces us that we are too small, weak, or inadequate to make a meaningful impact. It causes us to shrink back when we should step forward, keeping us stuck in the shadows of mediocrity when God calls us to step into the light of greatness.

It causes us to shrink back when we should step forward, keeping us stuck in the shadows of mediocrity when God calls us to step into the light of greatness.

Your self-perception—how you see yourself—is crucial to fulfilling your purpose. Think about it: how many brilliant ideas have you set aside because you doubted your abilities? When you view yourself through a lens of inadequacy, you limit your potential and may even turn away from the incredible opportunities God meant for you!

This is where I introduce Gideon, who saw himself as weak, inconsequential, and inadequate. We meet him threshing wheat in a winepress. In a winepress! Not the threshing floor, in the winepress, hiding from the Midianites to keep his harvest from being stolen. This was the act of a man gripped by fear, not of a bold or courageous leader. If you and I were in God's place, we might have been disappointed in him for not recognising

his potential. But God never gives up on us, even when we give up on ourselves.

In a moment that must have been both disturbing and intense, the Angel of the Lord appeared to Gideon and declared, "Mighty man of valour!" Can you picture Gideon's reaction? The shock, the disbelief? I can almost see him looking around, bewildered, wondering who else the angel could be addressing. "Me? A mighty warrior? Does this angel not see how insignificant I am?" he must have thought.

But that was the day he discovered his true self. The Gideon he recognized (the one he was accustomed to seeing in the mirror) was not who God intended him to be. Remember how he described himself? He stated he was the least important member of his family, and his clan was the weakest in the tribe of Manasseh (Judges 6:15). How could he be the one chosen to save Israel? But that was not how God viewed him. The Lord saw him as great and powerful. He acknowledged him as someone who could make a difference, just as He sees you! In life, until you recognize the forces that exert power over you, you will remain unable to control them. Ask yourself: what shapes how you see yourself? Past criticisms? Societal expectations? The opinions of others? Or personal insecurities? Many of us are unknowingly hindered by these influences. We may downplay them, yet they govern our lives. They determine everything about us: where we go, how we think, who we engage with, and what we do! Recognizing and understanding these forces is essential for reclaiming our autonomy and achieving meaningful change. Self-perception is one of those powerful forces. If you believe you are incapable or unworthy, those beliefs will inevitably manifest in how you live your life. On the other hand, if you operate with a healthy self-perception, you will walk in boldness, purpose, and fulfillment.

As we navigate life, the people we surround ourselves with can significantly influence our journey. Keeping the wrong company can be harmful, while choosing the right company, including your own, is invaluable. I purposely added 'including your own' not because you can separate yourself from yourself, but because it's important to consider yourself as part of the company you keep. Just as you would choose positive and supportive people to be around, you should also ensure that your thoughts and self-talk are positive and supportive. However, this is a side note; I want to emphasize the importance of keeping company with God.

Being close to someone often leads to you adopting their viewpoint. The longer you keep company with them, the more you begin to see things from their perspective. It is reassuring to know that God is one of those we can have in our lives. Although He is God and reigns in power, we still have a friend in Him.

It is comforting to know that God is one of those we can have in our space. Although He is God and reigns in power, we still have a friend in Him.

Now, to state the obvious- God is God! He has a different perspective from ours. He said, *"For my thoughts are not your thoughts, neither are your ways my ways," declares the Lord. "As the heavens are higher than the earth, so are my ways higher than your ways and my thoughts than your thoughts"* (**Isaiah 55:8-9 NIV**). His thoughts are indeed different and higher than ours. He also said, *"For I know the thoughts that I think toward you, says the Lord, thoughts of peace and not of evil, to give you a future and a hope"* (**Jeremiah 29:11 NKJV**).

In God's eyes, you are good. He created everything and called it good; you need to know He sees more incredible goodness in you. You were made in His image; He placed His Spirit in you; you are precious, cherished, and valuable!

"For we are God's masterpiece. He has created us anew in Christ Jesus, so we can do the good things He planned for us long ago." **From Ephesians 2:10**, it is clear that we are valued much more than we tend to acknowledge. Hear the words used to describe us: masterpiece, created a new, capable of doing good things. God sees us this way. Why, then, do we often doubt our worth? It is time to embrace our values and live out the good things we are meant to do. That was what took Gideon from insignificance to greatness.

It's time for my story. I lived with the littleness syndrome, and sometimes, it still rears its head. I used to suffer from chronic self-doubt; thankfully, its effect on me has drastically reduced. Some decades ago, I lost a precious gift. Let me tell you how it happened. I had a gift of prophecy and usually felt a leading to prophesy. However, whenever I considered it, I thought, "I'm not as spiritual as the others—what if I get it wrong?" Instead of getting up to speak during our fellowships, I stayed quiet in the background or would write out the words I received in my heart and send them to the people in charge.

One day, at a large NIFES conference, I sensed God giving me a prophecy to declare. I felt too small, and my voice was too soft to address such a large crowd. Again, I resorted to writing it down. Someone delivered the prophecy just as I put the period at the end of the last sentence. It was almost exactly word for word! As soon as the person finished, I felt a strange sensation, like something leaving me. I suddenly became hollow and empty. For many years, I never received messages again. The littleness syndrome stifled my potential as a prophetess. I don't want that to happen to you. That is why I am writing and urging you to see yourself differently. Now, let's get into the issues.

Origins and Impact of the Littleness Syndrome: Where does the Littleness Syndrome come from?

The littleness syndrome arises from a combination of internal and external factors, including negative thoughts, words, and experiences, which plant seeds of doubt and insecurity in our hearts. Our family upbringing plays a significant role in shaping our self-perception. A critical or neglectful home environment can profoundly impact one's self-worth. Constant comparisons, harsh criticisms, or a lack of genuine affection can leave us feeling inadequate. These experiences can leave lasting scars, causing us to question our abilities and value for years. If you are a parent or planning to start a family soon, remember to be mindful of the atmosphere you create—ensure it fosters growth and well-being.

Cultural and social norms can also negatively influence our self-worth. The pressure to conform to specific standards of success, beauty, or behaviour can make us feel like we are perpetually falling short. It often appears that everyone else is thriving, moving forward, and achieving their goals while we struggle to keep up. Failing to meet these unrealistic expectations can lead to a debilitating sense of failure and inadequacy, prompting us to question our value and position in the world.

Moreover, past failures or rejections can exacerbate these feelings. Personal setbacks, mistakes, or disappointments can lead us to believe we are incapable or unworthy of success. When these experiences weigh heavily on our hearts, they can convince us that we do not deserve to achieve our dreams and goals. Reflect on what has influenced your sense of self-worth. Was it societal pressure or the feeling of not measuring up to others?

What are the Consequences of Living with Littleness Syndrome?

The littleness syndrome creates a ripple effect across all areas of our lives, often in ways we may not immediately recognize. Viewing ourselves through the lens of limitation incapacitates us and makes success in our endeavours—whether in business, relationships, academics, or other pursuits—more challenging. This persistent insecurity can be overwhelming; it feels like a heavy weight, pressing us down and preventing us from reaching our dreams. It drains our energy and motivation, leaving us trapped and unable to escape the cycle of inadequacy.

When we constantly feel inadequate, it can lead to chronic stress and anxiety, which, in turn, affects our physical health. I remember a time when I was so overwhelmed by feelings of inadequacy that I started experiencing frequent headaches. The continual strain made me tense, further impacting my overall well-being.

Consistently feeling inadequate erodes our self-esteem and self-worth. It becomes difficult to recognize and celebrate our achievements and strengths. I often downplayed my successes, attributing them to external factors rather than my abilities. This mindset hindered my ability to build on past achievements. What happened was that I always had to start from scratch, which set me back significantly.

Social interactions can become incredibly challenging under the weight of the littleness syndrome. I used to avoid networking opportunities for fear of judgment and rejection. Although my experience wasn't as severe, some people have been deeply affected by feelings of isolation and loneliness. The fear of not measuring up can cause us to retreat into our shells and miss out on the joy of shared experiences and meaningful relationships.

Naturally, finances can become another casualty of the littleness syndrome, and for me (and many women I know), this is the most painful aspect! The fear of failure and a lack of confidence have prevented us from pursuing better job opportunities or business ventures. I remember when a friend suggested we partner to open a school in Canada.

It seemed like an incredible idea, but I couldn't envision achieving it, so I declined. You know what? Augusta saw herself differently and went ahead.

As I write, her school has been established and is now five years old! I could go on and on; creativity and innovation also suffer when self-doubt takes hold. Decision-making becomes daunting, and community involvement and leadership roles can feel out of reach when we don't believe in our capabilities. Parenting and family dynamics can also be affected by the littleness syndrome. Parents struggling with these feelings might inadvertently pass on their insecurities to their children (something I almost did with my daughter), impacting the next generation's self-perception and confidence. Ultimately, the littleness syndrome can prevent us from living a fulfilling and joyful life. Notwithstanding all that I said, the most devastating consequence of the littleness syndrome is how it distances us from God's purpose.

We unconsciously limit what God can do through us when we believe we are not enough. Doubt clouds our vision, fear paralyzes our actions, and weakness undermines our confidence. It becomes challenging to hear His call or trust in His plans. You may find yourself resisting growth opportunities, dismissing your spiritual gifts, or assuming that His promises are meant for others but not for you. This disconnect robs us of the abundant life God intends for us, keeping us bound in fear instead of walking boldly in faith. The longer we hold onto this mindset and see ourselves wrongly, the more challenging it becomes to recognize and embrace the limitless potential God has placed within us. The most devastating consequence of the littleness syndrome is how it distances us from God's purpose for our lives. Break the cycle of littleness syndrome to see yourself differently.

1. **Recognising the Roots**

   Why it matters:

   As we've discussed, the Littleness Syndrome doesn't appear out of nowhere. We witness its effects because it has deep roots. These roots can be identified, uprooted, and eliminated. Until this is accomplished, negative patterns and limiting beliefs will continue to hinder our progress. By addressing these deeply rooted issues, we can replace them with empowering truths and positive behaviours, leading to lasting transformation and growth.

Action

Take a moment to reflect: What specific moments or experiences made you feel small or inadequate? Write them down. Then, pray for clarity and invite God to reveal areas where healing and renewal are needed in your heart. This isn't about dwelling on the past but about uprooting harmful beliefs so you can move forward.

Biblical Insight

Jeremiah 1:5 says, *"I knew you before I formed you in your mother's womb."* God goes more profound than the roots of your issues. He saw your value and purpose long before life's challenges tried to tell you otherwise.

2. **Redefining Your Identity in Christ**

   Why it matters

   Your mistakes, failures, or accomplishments don't shape your identity. It is defined by God, who created you for a unique purpose. When we allow negative self-perceptions to dominate, we walk in falsehood rather than the truth of who God says we are. Seeing yourself differently starts with accepting your identity as a child of God who is deeply loved and wonderfully made.

Action

Speak life over yourself daily. Use affirmations rooted in Scripture, such as *"I am God's masterpiece"* (**Ephesians 2:10**) or *"I am fearfully and wonderfully made"* (**Psalm 139:14**). Place these truths where you can see them often and repeat them until they become your reality.

Biblical Insight

Galatians 2:20 reminds us, *"It is no longer I who live, but Christ lives in me." When you live with Christ at the centre of your identity, the weight of inadequacy fades, and you can begin to see yourself through His eyes.*

3. **Challenging Negative Patterns**

   Why it matters

   Negative patterns—like doubting your worth, procrastinating out of fear, or comparing yourself to others—keep you stuck. These habits drain your energy, diminish your confidence, and stop you from stepping into your God-given potential. Breaking these cycles is necessary to move forward with purpose and clarity.

Action

Start small. Identify one harmful habit and replace it with a positive, faith-filled action. For example, if fear of failure keeps you from trying something new, set a simple goal and take a step toward it today. Celebrate progress, knowing that even small steps lead to significant victories.

Biblical Insight

2 Timothy 1:7 declares, *"For God has not given us a spirit of fear but of power, love, and self-discipline."* God equips you with everything you need to overcome fear and take courageous action.

4. **Renewing the Mind**

Why it matters

Self-perception can change. The way you see yourself and think shapes how you live. If your mind is filled with negativity, self-doubt, and lies, those thoughts will limit your ability to see yourself differently. Renewing the mind by the Word of God can fix that. It is done by intentionally replacing lies with God's truth.

Action

Commit to spending time daily in God's Word. When a negative thought arises, counter it with Scripture. For instance, if you think, "I'm not good enough," combat that lies with **Philippians 4:13**: *"I can do all things through Christ who strengthens me." Meditate on these truths until they take root in your heart.*

Biblical Insight

Romans 12:1-2 states, *"Therefore, I urge you, brothers and sisters, given God's mercy, to offer your bodies as a living sacrifice, holy and pleasing to God—this is your true and proper worship. Do not conform to the pattern of this world but be transformed by the renewing of your mind."* Transformation is possible. Allow God's Word to reshape your thoughts and align you with His plans.

5. **Embracing Transformation**

Why it matters

Seeing yourself differently is not a one-time event—it's an ongoing journey of growth, faith, and trust in God. As you embrace your identity in Christ and continue stepping into your purpose, you'll find that the negative self-concepts that once held you captive no longer have power over you.

Action

Celebrate your progress and keep moving forward. Journaling your journey can help you recognize how far God has brought you. Share your story with others struggling with similar challenges and encourage them with the hope you've found.

Biblical Insight

Philippians 1:6 assures us, *"And I am certain that God, who began the good work within you, will continue His work until it is finally finished."* Trust that God is faithfully transforming you into who He created you to be.

6. **Seeking Support and Encouragement**

   Why it matters

   Isolation can make the Littleness Syndrome feel overwhelming. Surrounding yourself with a godly community can give you strength, encouragement, and accountability. The people around you can remind you of God's promises and uplift you when you stumble, fall, or feel stuck.

Action

Be intentional about building relationships with mentors, friends, or small groups who share your faith and values. Share your struggles and victories openly and allow others to encourage and challenge you. Seek prayer partners who will stand with you in faith.

Biblical Insight

Ecclesiastes 4:9-10 reminds us, *"Two people are better off than one, for they can help each other succeed. If one person falls, the other can reach out and help."* We're not designed to do life alone—God places people in our lives to walk alongside and lift us, too.

7. **Learning to Love Yourself**

Why it matters

Self-loathing is a silent thief; it robs you of joy, confidence, and the ability to see yourself as God does. When you fail to love yourself, it affects everything! Loving yourself allows you to embrace the unique way God has made you and live with greater peace and purpose. Loving yourself as God does is essential for accepting good, bad, and ugly. Then, you value yourself and break free from insecurity and unhealthy comparisons.

Action

Appreciate who God made you to be. Speak positively about yourself, practice self-care, and focus on your strengths. Surround yourself with encouraging people and thank God for His work in you.

Biblical Insight

"*Love your neighbour as yourself*" (**Mark 12:31**) begins with healthy self-love. Psalm 139:14 reminds us that we are fearfully and wonderfully made. Embrace God's truth and honour His creation by loving yourself.

Conclusion

Returning to Gideon, his story reminds us that God doesn't see us for who we are now but for whom He gave us the capacity to become through Him. Gideon's journey from fear and self-doubt to a bold, victorious leader teaches us the importance of seeing ourselves as He does.

God doesn't see us for who we are now but for whom He gave us the capacity to become through Him.

So, take heart from Gideon's story. Recognize that God sees your potential, even when you don't. Stop viewing yourself as the devil wants you to, and start seeing yourself as God desires, as a mighty person of valour!

Much love!

About the Author

Manuela Izunwa is a pastor, coach, and leadership trainer who empowers women to find clarity, confidence, and conviction. After overcoming self-doubt and a distorted self-image through God's truth, she now helps others do the same. With a PhD. in Leadership Development and diverse experience, she leads *ThriveWell Initiative*, *Deborah's Cradle*, and *GOLD*, mentoring thousands of women and girls.

She serves alongside her husband, Pastor George Izunwa, at *Gateway International Church,* living between Nigeria and the United Kingdom. Her mission is to equip others to boldly embrace their identity and purpose.

CHAPTER 22

VALUING RELATIONSHIP MORE

Relationships are the currency of life. Where money falls short, relationships yield results and open doors that were once closed, mainly when supported by the one who never fails: Almighty God. God ordained it from the beginning for us to have relationships. The command "be fruitful" is built on relationships, and as the saying goes, it takes two to tango. We can't go through life alone; we will always need people. We can't exist in a vacuum.

To truly live, we must engage in relationships and connect with others. We must wear clothes, eat food, wear shoes, travel, and utilize many things others produce—essentially, everything is interconnected. Life is much easier because of relationships.

It is fair to say that relationships are the currency of life, and a quick word of advice: spend it wisely.

What do we mean by Relationship?

Relationships refer to how two or more people or things are connected. They describe how individuals or groups regard or behave towards one another. Relationships include landlord/tenant, husband/wife, employee/employer, and neighbours within a community.

"Can two people walk together without agreeing on the direction?" **Amos 3:3 NLT** illustrates that relationships flourish when there is compliance, agreement, and a willingness to submit to one another.

Jesus emphasised the importance of relationships when he said, *"I am the Vine; you are the branches.* When you're joined with me and I with you, the relationship is intimate and organic— the harvest is sure to be abundant. Separated, you can't produce anything. Anyone who separates from me is deadwood, gathered up and thrown on the bonfire. But if you make yourselves at home with me and my words are in you, you can be sure that whatever you ask will be listened to, and Father reveals His nature when you bear grapes and grow as my disciples.

John 15:5-8 MSG

"Remain in me, and I will remain in you. For a branch cannot bear fruit if it is severed from the vine, and you cannot be fruitful unless you abide in me. Yes, I am the vine; you are the branches. Those who abide in me, and I in them, will produce much fruit. For apart from me, you can do nothing."

John 15:4-5 NLT

These scriptures highlight the significance of relationships in our lives today. The Lord Jesus, speaking there, further confirms that since the beginning, God has established everything based on relationships. Relationships must be valued and treated to get the most out of life. The scripture illustrates how relationships function and how they can fail.

The roles of the vine and the branch are illustrated. Abiding in me is your responsibility as a branch.

My role as the Vine is to ensure that you produce much fruit.

No matter where the branch is located on the tree or its size, as long as it is connected to the vine, it will flourish and bear fruit. If cut off or partly dislocated, it won't be like the others nor reach its maximum potential.

This exemplifies relationships in action; the command to be fruitful is grounded in the premise of relationships. Being fruitful means being relational—whether with God, your spouse, family, community, church, etc.

Everything advances or multiplies based on relationships. Relationships are connections that, when valued, can be advantageous because they are much more valuable than money. They can be spent like money in business, family, community, etc., and where money fails, relationships can open doors (or lead to closed doors when handled disdainfully).

Valuing relationships involves being selfless, contributing to one another's growth, supporting one another, avoiding backbiting and malicious talk, and steering clear of offense, to name a few.

The Lord makes it very clear in Ephesians that a key way to value relationships is to be selfless, humble, and gentle, and allow for each other's faults.

"And further, submit to one another out of reverence for Christ." **(Ephesians 5:21 NLT)**

"Always be humble and gentle. Be patient with each other, making allowances for each other's faults because of your love." **(Ephesians 4:2 NLT**)

Being courteous means being polite, respectful, or considerate. Relationships involve submission to each other and form organically, without manipulation or force. They develop naturally over time and are genuine and authentic. We become selfless out of love. That's why we emphasize being selfless and loving in relationships.

Because of Christ, we submit to one another. For a relationship to work, we must set aside our interests and love each other as Christ has shown us.

Examining the workings of relationships at various levels—family, marriage, church, social, career, business, and government—it becomes clear that there must be a willingness to submit to one another while being courteous, humble, and gentle and making allowances for others' faults; otherwise, it simply won't work.

In valuing relationships, God outlined roles and responsibilities for each party involved. For instance, in **John 15:4-5**, the roles and responsibilities are made clear: "*Abide in me*" means value this relationship, treat me right, and don't abandon or render me irrelevant; then, I will abide in you. If you seek to be fruitful, abide in me. The vine that does not abide will be cut off.

A body organ that does not respond to the brain's instructions begins to malfunction and eventually fails.

Listen to the instructions: wives submit, husbands love, the branch and vine relationship, parents don't provoke your children, obey the government because God has established it, respect leadership, etc. These are all God's ways of telling us to value relationships to get the best out of life. That is just how life is—it is built around relationships; you cannot navigate life alone, brothers and sisters. You need to value relationships to flourish and gain the best from life.

Many doors can be opened to you effortlessly because of relationships. There have been countless instances where what people have pursued for months or years falls into the laps of others due to strong relationships. This is why treating people well and engaging with everyone humbly and courteously is as crucial as being intentional about developing and nurturing relationships. You never know what doors may open through a chance encounter today, but if not handled properly, it can lead to doors being shut against you. Being skilled and knowledgeable is essential, but how you value and treat the people God brings your way significantly impacts your progress. We must be intentional regarding our relationships.

It takes hard work; a good example is a marital relationship. Following God's guidance and directives, we must be determined to make it work. Marriage is about two individuals coming together to become one despite their cultural, temperamental, and familial differences. This can only be achieved through selfless love, submission, forgiveness, overlooking mistakes, forbearance, and tolerance.

In valuing relationships, the following should be prioritised:

Communication involves intentionally being open and honest in sharing your thoughts and feelings. For communication to be effective, you must also be willing to listen to your partner (feelings, ideas, and needs) in a careful way. Effective communication will help everyone involved in a relationship understand each other clearly, resolve their issues more efficiently, and support one another better. Trust is another vital component in relationships and will help people feel safe with you and vice versa. This leads to mutual respect. Trust is cultivated through consistent actions and dealing with one another honestly and reliably.

Respect is about valuing other people's individuality, opinions, and boundaries. When you value relationships, you treat the other person equally and appreciate their uniqueness and perspectives. This will help others grow and strengthen your relationship.

Forgiveness... The scripture below encourages us to make allowances for each other's faults. There will always be reasons to disagree or offend, but we must learn to forgive each other, knowing we are imperfect. Forgiving one another demonstrates that we value the relationship and fulfill God's command to forgive one another.

"Always be humble and gentle. Be patient, allowing for each other's faults because of your love."

Ephesians 4:2 NLT

Appreciating one another and the efforts made are also significant in relationships, as they help focus on the positive aspects. This makes the other party feel valued and reinforces positive behaviours.

Loyalty, which may involve showing support and working together to resolve issues or overcome obstacles, is an excellent way to value relationships and reflect commitment.

In conclusion, a relationship must be nurtured intentionally for it to flourish. Remember, relationships are the currency of life. Please spend it wisely. Value your relationships, and work hard to keep them alive and thriving. The rewards are unlimited and can far exceed your expectations. Also, remember that wonderful things come in small packages; you never know what opportunities may arise from a chance encounter with someone, so treat everyone you meet with respect and demonstrate that you value the encounter.

The little slave girl was able to refer Naaman, a Syrian army general with leprosy, to the prophet Elisha because of how she was treated within the family, and that was how he received his healing. Don't look down on anyone or trivialize encounters with people. Whenever you meet someone or are in any relationship—employee/employer, neighbours, family members, church members, etc.—always ask yourself these questions: Why am I in this relationship? Why has God allowed us to meet? What am I to learn or impart to others in this relationship? Treat everyone respectfully, be trustworthy, and pray to God for guidance.

References

Bible Gateway.com (2011), The Bible New Living Translation (Online). Available at: https://www.biblegateway.com/versions/New-Living-Translation-NLT-Bible/#booklist

Bible Gateway.com (2011), The Bible Message Translation (Online). Available at: https://www.biblegateway.com/versions/Message-MSG-Bible/#booklist

About The Author

Olaronke Olayemi-Hassan is an Associate Pastor, entrepreneur, and community advocate. She co-founded *Rivers of Joy*, a social enterprise that transforms lives through faith-based outreach. She's also the founder of *Cakesbybonkus Ltd.*, a bespoke cake business. Olaronke has received several awards for her leadership, including the Borough Recognition Award.

She serves as a spiritual adviser and oversees a food bank, distributing groceries and clothing to those in need. With a background in banking and NHS governance, Olaronke is committed to building meaningful relationships and serving others. She's married with children and dedicated to purpose and service.

Chapter 23

HOW YOUR HABITS SHAPE YOUR PERSONALITY

Introduction

Habits are the small, often unconscious actions we repeat regularly, forming the foundation of our daily routines. They encompass everything from starting our day and interacting with others to our health, work, and leisure choices. While habits are typically viewed as mundane, they profoundly shape our personality and overall identity. Understanding the relationship between habits and personality provides insight into how our behaviours contribute to developing our character and individuality.

The Formation of Habits

Habits are developed through a process known as habit formation, which includes three main components: cue, routine, and reward. Charles Duhigg famously described this process in his book The Power of Habit.

1. **Cue:** This is the trigger that starts the habit. It can be an external event, a specific time of day, an emotional state, or a preceding routine. For instance, the cue for a morning coffee habit might be waking up.

2. **Routine:** refers to the actual behaviour or action following the cue. In the case of morning coffee, the routine involves brewing and drinking the coffee.

3. **Reward:** This is the positive outcome or benefit of completing the routine. For the coffee habit, the reward might be a boost in energy and the enjoyment of the drink.

Over time, as the cue-routine-reward loop is repeated, the habit becomes ingrained in our daily lives. Habits are reinforced by their rewards, which increase the likelihood of repetition. This reinforcement shapes our behaviour patterns and, consequently, our personality traits.

Habits and Personality Traits

Personality is often defined by consistent patterns of thoughts, feelings, and behaviours over time and across different situations. Since habits are repeated behaviours, they can significantly influence the development of personality traits.

1. **Work Ethics and Discipline**
   Work and discipline habits shape personality. Punctuality, diligence, and organization contribute to a reliable character. Conversely, procrastination and disorganization lead to irresponsibility and unreliability, which can negatively impact relationships.

2. **Social Interactions and Empathy**
   Regular habits in social interactions shape personality. Engaging in active listening, showing empathy, and expressing gratitude fosters kindness, openness, and warmth. Conversely, interrupting conversations, being

dismissive, or neglecting social niceties can lead to traits perceived as aloofness or insensitivity. Our habitual interactions influence how we are perceived and the relationships we form.

3. **Health and Well-being**
   Habits related to health and well-being have a direct impact on personality. Regular exercise, a balanced diet, and sufficient sleep contribute to physical health, affecting mental and emotional stability. Healthy habits often correlate with an energetic, resilient, and optimistic personality. For instance, individuals who exercise regularly may be more inclined to exhibit self-discipline and a positive outlook due to the endorphins and increased energy levels associated with physical activity.

   Conversely, poor diet, lack of exercise, and insufficient sleep can lead to negative personality traits. Individuals who regularly engage in unhealthy behaviours might struggle with fatigue, irritability, and low self-esteem, which can manifest as moodiness, pessimism, or a lack of motivation.

4. **Learning and Growth**

   Habits of continuous learning and personal growth shape personality by fostering traits like curiosity, open-mindedness, and adaptability. Engaging in reading and seeking new experiences contributes to a growth-oriented mindset. Conversely, resisting new experiences may lead to a more rigid and less adaptable personality.

The Role of Conscious Habits in Personality Development

While many habits are formed unconsciously, there is significant potential for consciously forming habits to intentionally shape one's personality. By being aware of the habits we want to develop, we can work towards reinforcing behaviours that align with the personality traits we aspire to cultivate.

1. **Goal Setting and Self-Improvement**

   Engaging in self-improvement habits like setting and reviewing personal goals can nurture ambition, perseverance, and self-discipline. Similarly, self-reflection and mindfulness can develop empathy, patience, and resilience, contributing to a well-rounded personality.

2. **Building Positive Relationships**
   Consciously cultivating habits that enhance relationships, such as regular communication, active listening, and expressing appreciation, can positively shape personality. These habits contribute to traits such as empathy, reliability, and warmth, which are valuable in personal and professional relationships. By prioritizing these habits, individuals can strengthen their social connections and foster a supportive and caring personality.

3. **Adapting to Change**
   Habits related to adaptability and openness to change are crucial for personal growth and personality development. Consciously developing habits that embrace new experiences, challenge existing beliefs, and adapt to changing circumstances can foster flexibility, resilience, and open-mindedness. These habits enable individuals to navigate life's uncertainties gracefully and maintain a positive attitude toward change.

The Impact of Habit Change on Personality

Changing habits can have a profound impact on personality. By altering habitual behaviours, individuals can influence their character traits and overall identity. For example, someone who habitually practices mindfulness and meditation may experience shifts in personality leading to greater calmness and emotional stability. Similarly, regular physical exercise can increase energy levels and a positive outlook.

1. **Overcoming Negative Habits**
   Addressing and overcoming negative habits is an essential aspect of personal development. Harmful habits, such as excessive procrastination, unhealthy eating, or chronic negativity, can shape personality traits that are counterproductive to personal and professional growth. Individuals can foster discipline, optimism, and resilience by consciously replacing these negative habits with positive alternatives.

   For instance, replacing the habit of procrastination with a habit of setting and adhering to deadlines can lead to traits associated with reliability and productivity.

Similarly, replacing negative self-talk with affirmations and positive reinforcement can contribute to a more positive and self-assured personality.

2. **Reinforcing Positive Habits**
   Reinforcing positive habits is equally crucial for personality development. By consistently practicing behaviours that align with desired personality traits, individuals can solidify these traits into their character. For example, regularly practicing gratitude and generosity can reinforce traits of kindness and empathy. Engaging in lifelong learning and curiosity can foster intellectual openness and adaptability.

Conclusion

Habits are more than mere routines; they are foundational elements that shape our personality and identity. By forming and reinforcing habits, individuals cultivate traits such as discipline, empathy, resilience, and adaptability. By consciously choosing and nurturing positive habits, individuals can meaningfully influence their personal growth and character development.

Understanding the interplay between habits and personality highlights the power of everyday actions in shaping who we are. Individuals can transform their personalities and identity by adopting new habits, modifying existing ones, or eliminating negative behaviours. As such, habits are crucial in personal development and self-improvement, offering a pathway to a more fulfilling and authentic life. one's personality.

On the other hand, putting things off and being disorganized can make you seem unreliable. If you often delay tasks and struggle with organization, you might be seen as inconsistent, affecting your professional and personal relationships.

Understanding how habits and personality interact reveals how our everyday actions shape our identity. Whether we adopt new habits, change old ones, or stop negative behaviours, we can change who we are over time. This makes habits essential for personal growth and self-improvement, leading to a more fulfilling life."

About the Author

Olutunu Babalola-Daniel encountered God as a committed Christian 37 years ago. She is an intercessor, a teacher of the word, and a worshiper.

Over the years, Olutunu has assisted and pioneered church planting projects and worked as a bible-study teacher, youth leader, church administrator, treasurer, and trustee. Olutunu is passionate about pulling down strongholds and seeing captives set free from Satan's Kingdom through intense prayers. '*The Arsenal of the Christian*' is Olutunu's first writing project. In this book, she has used her life experiences to explore all the weapons the Lord has equipped every believer with for living a spirit-filled and purposeful life.

Olutunu currently attends *RCCG Impact Centre Church* in Bicester. She is married to Rotimi Patrick Daniel.

CHAPTER 24

ADULTIFICATION AND ITS IMPACT ON LEARNING

Have you ever noticed how some children seem to bear the world's weight on their shoulders? They act more mature than they are in their years, taking on inappropriate responsibilities for their age. This phenomenon is known as adultification—when children are expected to adopt roles or behaviors typically associated with adults.

While it may seem complimentary to say a child is "so mature for their age," the reality of adultification is far more complex and can significantly impact a child's mental health, especially regarding their education.

What is Adultification?

Adultification happens when children are pushed into roles of responsibility or maturity before they're emotionally, mentally, or physically ready. It often occurs in households where parents or caregivers cannot fulfil their roles due to financial struggles, illness, or other life challenges.

There are two main types of Adultification

1. **Precocious Adultification**
   This involves children taking on adult-like roles, such as caring for siblings, managing household tasks, or even confiding in a parent.

2. **Cultural Adultification**
   This occurs when societal or cultural expectations impose adult-like responsibilities or behaviours on children. For example, children from minority communities may be expected to navigate systemic challenges or act as translators for their families in unfamiliar systems.

While these experiences might seem to build resilience, adultification can deprive children of their childhood, leading to long-term consequences.

The Pressure of Being "The Responsible One"

Imagine being a child who wakes up not thinking about school or play but about whether the bills have been paid or if there's enough food in the fridge. This is the reality for many children who experience adultification. In these situations, children often feel a sense of responsibility far beyond their years. While their peers are worried about homework or playground drama, these children deal with adult concerns.

This added responsibility can create a constant state of stress. For a child, the home should ideally be a place of safety and support, where they can relax and recharge. When home becomes a source of pressure, it can take a toll on their mental health. They might feel anxious, overwhelmed, or even guilty if they fail to meet these adult expectations.

The Impact on Mental Health

Adultification can have a profound impact on a child's mental health. Here are some of the common effects:

1. **Anxiety and Stress**
   Constantly worrying about adult responsibilities can leave children feeling anxious and stressed. They may struggle to sleep, concentrate, or enjoy activities that bring them joy.

2. **Low Self-Esteem**
   When children are given responsibilities they're not equipped to handle, they might internalise feelings of failure or inadequacy. This can lead to low self-esteem that follows them into adulthood.

3. **Depression**
   The emotional burden of adultification can leave children feeling isolated and unsupported, which can contribute to depression. They might feel like they have no one to turn to because they're expected to be "the strong one."

4. **Difficulty Forming Relationships**
   Adultified children often struggle to relate to peers because their experiences and priorities differ. This can lead to social isolation or difficulties forming meaningful connections.

How Adultification Affects Education

The classroom is often where the effects of adultification become most apparent. School is not just a place for learning but also a source of pressure for adultified children. Here's how adultification can impact their education:

Struggles with Focus and Engagement: When a child is preoccupied with adult concerns, focusing on schoolwork is challenging. Teachers might see them as distracted or uninterested, but their mental bandwidth is thin.

Difficulty Asking for Help
Adultified children are often used to caring for others, so they might struggle to ask for help when needed. They might fear being seen as weak or feel like they should be able to handle things independently.

Underperformance or Overachievement: Some adultified children may struggle academically because they're overwhelmed, while others might become overachievers, using academic success to compensate for their lack of control in other areas of their lives.

Behavioural Issues

The stress and frustration of adultification can sometimes manifest as behavioural issues in the classroom. These children might act out, withdraw, or appear uncooperative, which can lead to misunderstandings with teachers and peers.

Breaking the Cycle

So, what can be done to support adultified children and help them reclaim their childhood? It starts with recognising the signs and creating environments where they feel supported and understood.

1. **At Home**

   Set Boundaries: While it's essential for children to learn responsibility, there's a difference between age-appropriate chores and taking on adult roles. Caregivers should be mindful of what they ask of their children.

Create Open Communication: Let children express their feelings without fear of judgment. Acknowledge their efforts and reassure them that being a child is okay.

Seek Support: If a family is struggling, seeking help from the community organisations, counsellors, or social services can relieve some pressure on the child.

2. **In Schools**

   Train Teachers to Recognise Adultification: Educators should be aware of the signs of adultification and understand how it impacts children's behaviour and learning.

   Provide Emotional Support: Schools can offer counselling services or peer support groups to help adultified children feel less alone.

   Foster a Nurturing Environment: Simple acts like showing empathy, offering encouragement, or being patient can make a difference.

3. **As a Society**

   Address Systemic Issues: Many instances of adultification stem from more significant societal problems like poverty, discrimination, and lack of access to resources. Addressing these root causes can help reduce the burden on families and, in turn, children.

   Challenge Cultural Norms: In some cultures, adultification is normalised. Raising awareness about its impact can help shift these expectations and protect children's well-being.

Final Thoughts

Adultification is often an invisible burden that too many children carry without anyone realising it. While it might teach resilience in some ways, it also comes at a significant cost to their mental health and development. By recognising the signs and taking steps to support these children, we can help them find balance and ensure they can thrive—both in the classroom and beyond. After all, childhood is a time for exploration, learning, and joy. Every child deserves the chance to experience it fully, without the weight of adult responsibilities holding them back.

I have learned that God is faithful and always has our best interests at heart, even when He allows us to face trials.

About the Author

Eliyo Ajiboye is the CEO of *Wisdom Tree Communities CIC*, a social enterprise empowering parents to navigate the United Kingdom education system. Through culturally responsive training, advocacy, and community events, she equips families with the tools to engage confidently with schools and improve outcomes for children.

CHAPTER 25

STRONG CONNECTIONS MAKE LIFE RICHER

The Values of the Mother-Daughter Relationship

Introduction

The relationship between a mother and daughter is one of the most complex, deeply rooted, and emotionally charged connections in human experience. Spanning the full spectrum of love, conflict, nurture, and transformation, this bond often acts as both a mirror and a map reflecting identity while guiding growth. Across cultures, generations, and histories, the mother-daughter relationship has served as a cornerstone of familial and societal structure. The values embedded within this relationship are powerful: love, empathy, sacrifice, identity formation, communication, strength, resilience, and legacy. This essay delves into the profound significance of these values and examines how they shape not only the individuals involved but the communities and cultures they inhabit.

The Foundation: Unconditional Love and Nurture

At its core, the mother-daughter relationship is often built on a foundation of unconditional love. From the moment of birth, a mother typically becomes the first source of safety, comfort, and sustenance. For many daughters, the mother is the first teacher, the first friend, and the first example of womanhood. This love is not merely sentimental; it is functional. It teaches trust, emotional security, and the ability to form healthy attachments with others.

Even in challenging relationships, where the expression of love may be complicated by circumstances, the underlying desire for connection often remains intact. This emotional undercurrent of nurture gives rise to resilience in daughters and deepens the capacity for compassion in mothers. When unconditional love is present, it becomes the bedrock upon which all other values are built.

Empathy and Emotional Intelligence

One of the most critical values nurtured within the mother-daughter bond is empathy. Because this relationship is typically so emotionally intimate, it provides a rich environment for developing emotional intelligence.

A daughter learns to interpret facial expressions, tone of voice, and unspoken cues. She witnesses emotional responses and begins to model or challenge them. Mothers who share their vulnerabilities who cry in front of their daughters, or apologize after conflict teach valuable lessons about emotional honesty and human imperfection.

Conversely, daughters who grow up witnessing only suppression or volatility may either adopt those behaviors or consciously work to break those cycles. In either case, the relationship serves as a laboratory for emotional learning.

Empathy becomes not just a skill but a moral compass. Daughters who have been taught, either directly or by example, to care about how others feel, are more likely to become thoughtful partners, engaged citizens, and nurturing parents in their own right.

The Power of Communication

Healthy mother-daughter relationships often hinge on communication. The way a mother communicates with her daughter can set the tone for how the daughter views herself and the world. Constructive communication marked by listening, validating, and encouraging expression can foster self-esteem and agency. On the other hand, communication filled with criticism, silence, or judgment can create wounds that take years to heal.

However, it is essential to recognize that communication is a skill that can evolve. As daughters grow into adolescents and adults, they may begin to communicate their needs, boundaries, and ideas more assertively. This shift can cause tension, but it also opens the door to mutual understanding and respect.

When both mother and daughter learn to speak and listen with intention, they create a safe space for growth, change, and reconnection. This space can become sacred ground a place where difficult truths are met with compassion rather than defensiveness.

Identity and Individuality

The mother-daughter relationship also plays a vital role in shaping identity. Daughters often look to their mothers for clues about womanhood, self-worth, and social roles. Mothers, knowingly or not, model what it means to live with strength, vulnerability, independence, or dependence. These lessons can be empowering or limiting, depending on the nature of the relationship and the values being transmitted.

As daughters mature, they often enter a stage of differentiation—seeking to define themselves apart from their mothers. This can be a time of friction but also one of growth. A healthy relationship allows space for individuality. A mother who honors her daughter's uniqueness—even when it diverges from her own worldview—plants the seeds for mutual respect.

Identity development is not a one-way street. Mothers, too, can evolve through their relationships with their daughters.

Daughters may challenge their mothers to question old beliefs, embrace new perspectives, or revisit dreams once put aside. This reciprocal evolution underscores the dynamic nature of the bond.

Strength and Sacrifice

The mother-daughter relationship is often marked by incredible strength and sacrifice. Mothers make countless sacrifices emotional, physical, financial to support their daughters. From sleepless nights to career compromises, these acts of giving are often done without fanfare. Such sacrifices model a form of love that is both fierce and selfless.

However, strength in this relationship does not lie in martyrdom alone. It lies in perseverance, in showing up through conflict and misunderstanding. It lies in being a safe harbor during a daughter's storms and a guiding light during her journeys. For daughters, strength may manifest in advocating for themselves, setting boundaries, or choosing different paths than those modelled.

Understanding and appreciating these sacrifices and recognizing when they come at a cost can create empathy between mother and daughter. It can also open conversations about shared responsibility, self-care, and generational healing.

Generational Wisdom and Legacy

The mother-daughter bond is a vessel for the transmission of generational wisdom. Cultural values, family traditions, spiritual beliefs, and life skills often pass from mother to daughter. Whether it's cooking a traditional meal, telling ancestral stories, or navigating social expectations, mothers serve as living repositories of knowledge.

This passing down of wisdom can be deeply grounding for daughters, helping them feel connected to a larger lineage. It also offers a sense of continuity in an often-fragmented world. However, this transmission is not always seamless. Daughters may reject or reinterpret the values they inherit, seeking to forge their own paths.

In doing so, they create a dynamic legacy—one that evolves rather than stagnates. Some of the most meaningful mother-daughter relationships are those in which both parties engage with legacy not as a script to follow but as a dialogue to co-create.

Conflict and Reconciliation

No meaningful relationship is without conflict, and the mother-daughter bond is no exception. Disagreements may stem from generational divides, differing values, life choices, or unresolved traumas. Yet, within conflict lies the potential for deeper understanding and transformation.

The value of reconciliation of coming back to the table with humility and open-heartedness is essential in sustaining this relationship. Mothers and daughters who are willing to admit fault, seek forgiveness, and commit to growth often come out stronger on the other side.

Reconciliation does not mean erasure of pain; rather, it is a recognition of shared humanity. It is a choice to prioritize love over pride, connection over control. When a mother and daughter choose each other after disagreement, they affirm the resilience of their bond.

Cultural Contexts and Social Influences

The mother-daughter relationship is deeply influenced by cultural norms and social expectations. In some cultures, daughters are expected to emulate their mothers closely, continuing traditions and fulfilling familial roles. In others, daughters are encouraged to forge their own paths, even if it means challenging parental authority.

These cultural dynamics can either enhance or complicate the relationship. For immigrant families, for instance, the mother-daughter bond may become a bridge—or a battleground—between the old world and the new. Daughters may serve as cultural interpreters for their mothers, while simultaneously navigating their own identities in unfamiliar terrain.

Understanding the social context of the relationship adds nuance to the values it embodies. It also invites empathy for the unique challenges faced by mothers and daughters who are navigating multiple cultural worlds.

Healing Across Generations

Many daughters carry the emotional residue of their mothers' unhealed wounds. Trauma, loss, and patterns of silence often ripple through generations. But just as pain can be passed down, so too can healing. When mothers acknowledge their own histories—of struggle, silence, or survival—they open the door for authentic connection.

Daughters who are willing to engage with their mothers' humanity—not just their roles—can shift entrenched dynamics. Therapy, storytelling, forgiveness, and honest dialogue become tools of transformation. Through this process, the mother-daughter relationship becomes a site of generational healing rather than generational harm.

Conclusion

The values of the mother-daughter relationship are vast, intricate, and deeply formative. Love, empathy, communication, identity, strength, legacy, and healing are not abstract ideals they are lived experiences that unfold in kitchens, hospitals, bedrooms, and phone calls. They are tested by conflict, reinforced by ritual, and redefined across time.

To honor the mother-daughter bond is to recognize its power not just in shaping individuals but in shaping societies. A daughter raised with love and self-worth becomes a woman who contributes meaningfully to her world. A mother who sees and values her daughter as a whole person contributes to a culture of dignity, equality, and emotional wisdom.

Ultimately, the mother-daughter relationship is not static. It is a living, breathing relationship that grows, contracts, breaks, and mends. Its values are not given—they are chosen, nurtured, and sometimes hard-won. But in its highest form, this relationship can be a source of profound beauty, wisdom, and transformation.

About the Author

Moreen Pattison is a dedicated charity CEO with a deep passion for education and social impact. Known for her professional leadership and commitment to meaningful change, she works to expand and empower communities through educational focussed initiatives.

CHAPTER 26

UPBRINGING LASTING EFFECT

Train up a child in the way he should go and when he is old, he will not depart from it.

Proverbs 22:6

This verse reveals the deep importance of upbringing. Instilling morals and values in children has long-term effects, whether positive or negative. Good training fosters strong, healthy relationships and shapes every aspect of life including interactions with people, money, work and self-worth.

You can often notice a child's foundation by observing their behaviour or speech. A good upbringing shapes not only actions but also learning and development. However, when the foundation is weak, the outcomes in adulthood may suffer. Still, there is always room for learning and change. The Bible asks, "If the foundation of the righteous is destroyed, what can the righteous do?" (Psalm 11:3). As for me, I will tear down the faulty foundation and rebuild it from scratch.

Early Impressions and Relationship Models

From birth, a child begins forming impressions based on their surroundings. Parents, siblings and extended family members become the first models for behaviour and relationships.

A child raised in an environment of love, affection and open communication tends to develop secure attachment styles and healthy relationships in adulthood. On the other hand, those raised in chaotic, neglectful or violent environments often form insecure attachments and struggle with relationships unless there is an intentional intervention.

Growing up in a loving Christian home where affection was freely shown and communication was encouraged, helped my siblings and I flourish. Correction was also part of our growth. As the Bible advises, “He who spares the rod hates his son” (Proverbs 13:24). My father used words, while my mother’s actions were unforgettable.

Attachment Styles and their Long-Term Effects

Ever wonder why some people always end up in toxic relationships despite deliverances or prayers? A deeper look at childhood attachment patterns often provides answers.

According to John Bowlby and Mary Ainsworth’s attachment theory, our early relationships shape our thinking, feeling and behaviour in adult relationships. These patterns, if unaddressed, may cause dysfunction. The four main attachment styles include:

Secure Attachment: Individuals feel comfortable with intimacy and independence. They are emotionally intelligent, trust easily, communicate effectively and maintain healthy boundaries. They thrive in various aspects of life without needing external validation.

Anxious Attachment: These individuals are often insecure and fear abandonment. They seek validation and approval and may remain in unhealthy relationships due to low self-worth. They often view themselves negatively and are overly dependent on others.

Avoidant Attachment: These individuals avoid emotional closeness, suppress their feelings and see themselves as independent. They struggle with vulnerability and tend to withdraw when someone gets too close.

Disorganized Attachment: This style is a mix of anxious and avoidant behaviours. It often stems from unresolved trauma and inconsistent caregiving. People with this attachment style may struggle with emotional regulation and fear intimacy.

Understanding your attachment style is crucial. It helps identify root causes and begin healing through therapy, counselling or other forms of emotional support.

The Role of Family as Social Models

Family is the primary place for social learning. Children mimic the behaviour of parents and caregivers. Positive role models who practice empathy, respect and effective communication set a solid foundation for future relationships.

However, negative models may result in dysfunction. Children who witness parental conflict, abuse or dishonesty may adopt these patterns in their own relationships. Some parents assume children are unaware of their actions, but children often sense more than adults realise.

Breaking free from toxic patterns requires intentional effort and sometimes professional guidance. A fruit does not fall far from the tree, but a determined person can choose a new path.

Effects of Parental Upbringing on Children

1. **Conflict Resolution and Communication Skills**
   Children who witness respectful communication and healthy conflict resolution learn to resolve disagreements through calm dialogue and compromise. They understand that conflict is natural and can be addressed maturely.

In contrast, children who witness aggression or avoidance may adopt those same unhealthy habits, leading to strained relationships. Learning to listen actively and express oneself respectfully helps to build better relationships.

2. **Fosters a Growth Mindset**

   Our upbringing influences how we view learning and challenges. Carol Dweck's "growth mindset" theory shows that believing in effort and persistence helps children embrace learning and personal growth.

   When parents praise effort rather than innate ability, children become resilient, embrace challenges and maintain a healthy self-image. A growth mindset develops from an early age and shapes a child's ability to learn, overcome setbacks and succeed.

3. **Adaptability and Resilience**

   Supportive upbringings help children develop resilience. They learn to view setbacks as opportunities and adapt positively to change. On the other hand, chaotic or unpredictable environments often lead to fear, emotional instability and poor coping mechanisms.

Children raised in instability may fear failure and resist taking risks, limiting their personal and professional growth. Building resilience often involves addressing past trauma and fostering emotional stability.

The Interplay between Relationship Management and Learning

Skills such as communication, resilience and conflict resolution are deeply interconnected. Strong communication improves teamwork and learning, while resilience helps individuals persist through challenges.

Children raised in nurturing homes often develop emotional awareness, set healthy boundaries and form positive relationships in school, work and community settings.

Learning through Relationships

Relationships teach us through exposure to different perspectives and life experiences. They challenge our thinking, expand our worldview and reinforce essential life skills.

Children raised in stable homes often possess emotional intelligence and can form boundaries while maintaining their values. They learn from others without losing themselves.

Breaking the Cycle

The first step toward healing is awareness. Recognising how your upbringing has shaped you allows you to begin the work of transformation. Healing may involve therapy, personal reflection and commitment to growth.

Practical Steps for Healing

1. **Self-Reflection**: Spend time reflecting on your upbringing. Identify the beliefs and behaviours you absorbed and how they affect your current life.

2. **Seek Support**: Therapy or counselling can provide tools to address trauma, develop healthier habits and manage relationships more effectively.

3. **Practice Communication**: Improve communication by listening actively, expressing yourself clearly and asking for clarification rather than reacting defensively.

4. **Embrace Challenges**: Adopt a growth mindset. Let go of limiting beliefs and view every challenge as an opportunity to learn and grow. Celebrate your effort, not just the results.

5. **Build Resilience**: Develop resilience by practicing self-care, setting realistic goals and learning from your experiences. Be kind to yourself and allow time for change.

6. **Practice Gratitude**: Focus on what is working in your life. Acknowledge your blessings and express gratitude. This reduces stress, improves focus and strengthens self-esteem.

Conclusion

Our upbringing plays a powerful role in shaping our beliefs, actions and relationships. A child's home environment affects how they relate to others, respond to conflict, embrace learning and manage emotions. Homes filled with love and discipline tend to raise confident, emotionally intelligent individuals. Conversely, homes marked by conflict and neglect can leave lasting wounds.

Many marriages affected by domestic violence trace their roots to dysfunctional upbringings. For the world to be better, families must recognise their role in shaping the next generation. They must learn how their leadership influences society and take steps to raise emotionally healthy children.

Even if your upbringing was less than ideal, there is hope. Healing and growth are possible at any stage of life. The journey may be long, but it is worth it. By investing in yourself and your relationships, you can break generational cycles and create a new legacy.

Now, you know your attachment style. Are you happy with it?

If your answer is no, what steps are you willing to take to improve yourself?

What personal development strategy will you put in place for your growth?

Children raised in nurturing homes often develop emotional awareness, set healthy boundaries and form positive relationships in school, work and community settings.

About the Author

Amara Ogba is a renowned faith-based leader, transformational coach, pastor, and singer-songwriter. She's the author of the UK #1 best-selling book *'Gratitude: Access for More'*. Amara serves as President of *Women on Their Knees International* and Lead Pastor of *The Honour Gate.* She also runs *The House of Honour Academy*, a women-only coaching and mentorship group.

With extensive academic credentials, including multiple master's degrees and certifications in coaching and NLP, Amara is a respected figure in her field. She's dedicated to helping others discover and fulfill their purpose through her coaching, mentorship, and ministry.